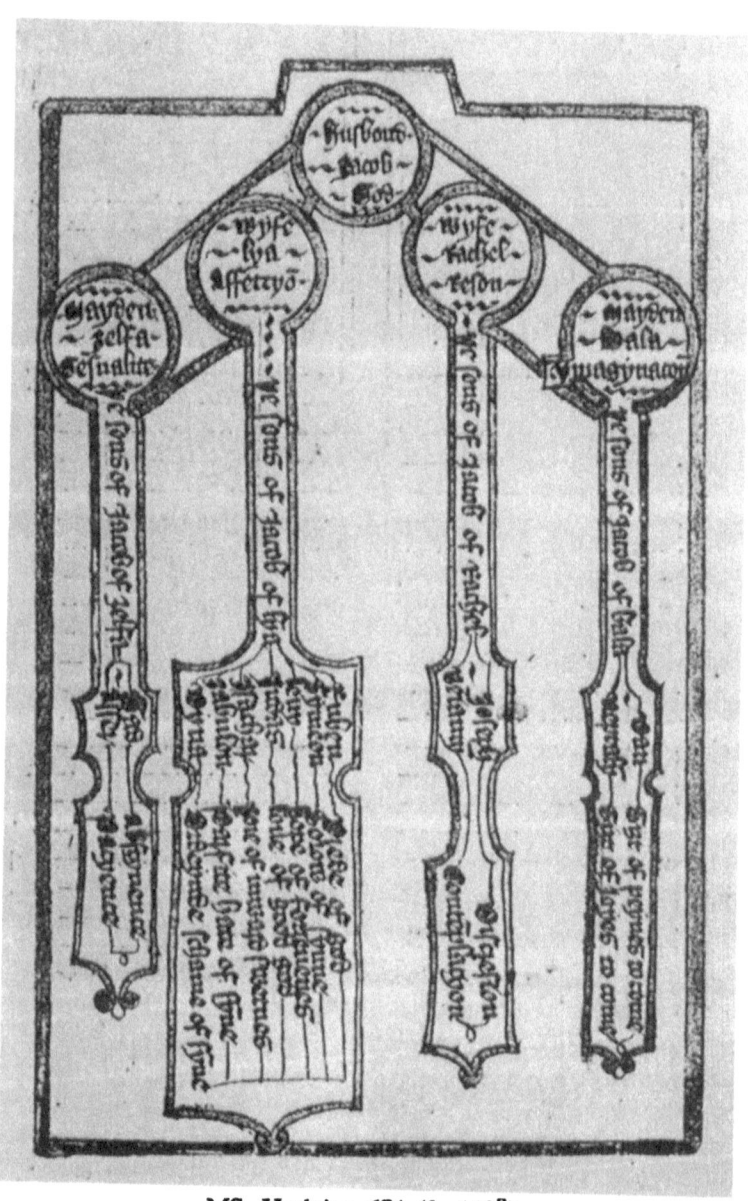

MS. Harleian 674 (f. 112ª)
By permission of the British Library

# RICHARD OF ST. VICTOR'S
# *TREATISE OF THE STUDY OF WISDOM THAT MEN CALL BENJAMIN*

## AS ADAPTED IN MIDDLE ENGLISH BY THE AUTHOR OF
## *THE CLOUD OF UNKNOWING*

Together with
*Treatise on Discretion of Spirits*
and
*Epistle on Discretion of Stirrings*

Translated, with Introductions and Notes
by
Dick Barnes

Studies in Mediaeval Literature
Volume 7

The Edwin Mellen Press
Lewiston/Queenston/Lampeter

Library of Congress Cataloging-in-Publication Data

Author of The cloud of unknowing, 14th cent.
    [Selections. English. 1990]
    Richard of St. Victor's Treatise of the study of wisdom that men call Benjamin : as adapted in Middle English ; together with Treatise on discretion of spirits ; and, Epistle on discretion of stirrings / by the author of The cloud of unknowing ; translated with introductions and notes by Dick Barnes.
    p. cm. -- (Studies in mediaeval literature ; v. 7 )
    Translation of the Middle English paraphrase of Richard of St. Victor's treatise Benjamin minor.
    ISBN 0-7734-0793-6
    1. Mysticism--History--Middle Ages, 600-1500. 2. Mysticism--England. I. Barnes, Dick, 1932- . II. Richard, of St. Victor, d. 1173. Benjamin minor. III. Title. IV. Title: Richard of Saint Victor's Treatise of the study of wisdom that men call Benjamin. V. Title: Treatise of the study of wisdom that men call Benjamin. VI. Series.
    BV5080.A8213  1990
    248.22--dc20                                              90-39519
                                                                  CIP

---

This is volume 7 in the continuing series
Studies in Mediaeval Literature
Volume 7
SML Series ISBN 0-88946-314-X

---

A CIP catalog record for this book
is available from the British Library.
Copyright © 1990 Dick Barnes

All rights reserved. For information contact

The Edwin Mellen Press　　　　　　　　　　The Edwin Mellen Press
Box 450　　　　　　　　　　　　　　　　　　Box 67
Lewiston, New York　　　　　　　　　　　　Queenston, Ontario
USA 14092　　　　　　　　　　　　　　　　　CANADA L0S 1L0

The Edwin Mellen Press, Ltd.
Lampeter, Dyfed, Wales
UNITED KINGDOM SA48 7DY

Printed in the United States of America

# RICHARD OF ST. VICTOR'S
## *TREATISE OF THE STUDY OF WISDOM*
## *THAT MEN CALL BENJAMIN*

### AS ADAPTED IN MIDDLE ENGLISH BY THE AUTHOR OF
### *THE CLOUD OF UNKNOWING*

Together with
*Treatise on Discretion of Spirits*
and
*Epistle on Discretion of Stirrings*

# TABLE OF CONTENTS

Introduction to Benjamin .................................................................................. 1
Old Testament Readings on the Twelve Patriarchs ......................................... 15
    The Births of Jacob's children (Genesis 29,30,35) ............................ 17
    Jacob's Blessing (Genesis 49) ............................................................ 22
    Moses' Blessing (Deuteronomy 33) ................................................... 24
A Treatise of the Study of Wisdom that Men Call Benjamin ........................... 27
A Note on Translation ...................................................................................... 49
Introduction to the Briefer Works .................................................................... 51
An Epistle on Discretion of Stirrings ............................................................... 57
A Treatise on Discretion of Spirits .................................................................. 71

# INTRODUCTION TO THE BENJAMIN

# INTRODUCTION TO THE BENJAMIN

This work came out of the practice of contemplation and was written to be used by those who wanted to practice it themselves. As prior of the abbey of St. Victor in the third quarter of the Twelfth Century, Richard directed novices in their spiritual exercises; no doubt his *Benjamin Minor, or On the Preparation of the Soul for Contemplation* was written for their instruction, and it shows by the depth and intricacy of its psychological insights that its author had been over the course more than once. A Middle English version of his treatise, composed in the latter part of the fourteenth century, was likewise made for use, in this case by the author's young "friend in God." It is a greatly condensed paraphrase that nevertheless includes the translator's own elaborations and separate insights. This version is the one I have tried to carry into our English. And while it's true that both the Latin and Middle English seem to me radiantly beautiful, characterized by a plainess, subtlety, humor, vigor, and shimmering simplicity that I find delightful; and true also that there is some intellectual and historical interest in the authors' understanding of our minds and of the Bible, as well as in their connections with other writers both earlier and later -- matters I intend to discuss as best I can in this introduction -- yet it still seems to me that the main interest of this present work, and the true source of its literary and historical interest, is its ability to nourish the spirit striving for an authentic life while still in this world.

The treatise is a quite straightforward account of the changing states of the soul as it cuts itself off from delusory joys and is brought by grace to the experience of real ones: something Richard and his Middle English translator had to know about from practice to write about with understanding. Yet it takes the form of a commentary on the passages in

Genesis that tell of the births of Jacob's twelve sons and his daughter, as if explaining what the Bible "meant" by them. This procedure will seem strange to a reader schooled in other modes of interpretation, but I believe Richard's way goes pretty well with the way the Bible got itself written. Seen from the inside, it makes sense.

For him the Bible was the record of divine revelations not too different from the ones he and others he knew or knew about had experienced themselves. Like St. Paul they were ravished to the third heaven and heard ineffable words not lawful for a man to utter:[1] a quite incommunicable experience, even an unintelligible one, yet so tremendously important that it needed to be told and understood. If something like that happens to you, you look around for other people who are supposed to have experienced like raptures, and you find that by various hints and oblique sayings you can define and test what you've been given or taught. Then you can take part in the conversation. For Richard, as for his master Hugh of St. Victor, the main test was the Bible (though of course they knew their Augustine and Gregory the Great and their dark Dionysius the Areopagite, and they had their own confessors, meditation masters, and spiritual friends in the community). In a passage of the *Benjamin Minor* not translated in the Middle English version Richard says that even if you've gone up onto the mountain apart and seen Christ transfigured you shouldn't be too ready to believe either what you see or what he says to you unless Moses and Elijah run to meet him: "I distrust any truth not confirmed by the authority of the Scriptures nor do I receive Christ in his clarification if Moses and Elijah are not with him." I believe he means by Moses and Elijah exactly what Matthew and Mark mean when they say that on the mount of Transfiguration the three disciples "saw Moses and Elijah talking with Jesus."[2] Moses and Elijah stand for, or are, the Law and the Prophets, the Torah and the rest of the Old Testament. The Bible writes itself along like *Finnegans Wake*, mentioning itself often in different ways. Ezekiel saw visions, Daniel interpreted dreams, their truth clarified John's visions on the island of Patmos. Jeremiah, the

---

1. II Cor. 12.2-4.
2. Matt. 17.1-13, Mark 9.2-9.

Psalms, Isaiah, are written newly in the Gospels. Even the Devil knew that: "If you're the Messiah, jump off this Temple, because it's written that the angels will carry you up so you won't even stub your toe on a rock."[3] It's not a matter of literary-historical influences so much as of shared witness recognized through time. Risen from the grave, Christ walked along the road with the disciples, and what he talked about was the Bible: "Beginning at Moses and all the prophets, he expounded to them in all the scriptures the things that were concerning him."[4]

In the Bible there are events whose connection to each other can be understood in what is for us the ordinary way, as cause and effect. Joshua blew the shofar, and down fell the wall. Others events are connected in a different way: they *mean* each other. Moses watches the battle from a hill, and notices that when he holds his arms out his side wins. The battle goes on so long that he gets two men to stand beside him, holding up his arms. The meaning of this figure is revealed on Golgatha, Jesus between the two thieves. And the meaning is reciprocal: like Moses, Christ crucified is somehow leading his people out of the slavery we suffered amidst the flesh pots, and because he is up there on the hill like that we are somehow victorious. When the sailors decide that Jonah is the cause of the storm they throw him into the sea where a fish swallows him. There he proves his faith by a psalm *de profundis*, and on the third day he is vomited safely onto the shore. This story has its own meaning but a different kind of meaning is revealed when Christ comes back from his two days among the dead: Jonah's story turns out to have been a prefiguration of that. If something of the sort happens to you it will be a postfiguration, and at that time you will have a different kind of access to the meaning of the other stories. If you are diligent, and blessed, you will be able to live the Book and read your life. Augustine at the crisis of his conversion, distractedly pacing in a garden, heard a child's voice say "Take and read," so he took up a scroll of Paul's epistles and read a verse at random. It swam up to his eye with what seemed

---

3. Matt. 4.5-7, Ps. 90.11-12/91.11-12. When the numbering of Psalm and verse differs between the Douai Version and the Authorized, I give both references, Douai first, separated by a slash.

4. Luke 24.27.

to him miraculous force and aptness, telling him clearly what was his to do: "In an instant, as I came to the end of the sentence, it was as though the light of confidence flooded into my heart and all the darkness of doubt was dispelled."[5] St. Anthony of Egypt, as Augustine remembered, had been converted in about the same way: he had gone into a church while a lesson was being read from the Gospel and had taken it as a direct message to himself. Augustine, calm for a change, told his friend Alupius what he had done, whereupon Alupius seized the scroll, read the next verse, and was converted too.

It's not lost on me that these ways of reading the Bible may sound absurd, or arbitrary, or pretentious, or worse: they may sound like the delusions of the schizophrenic, who also sees signs and may fasten on some spooky book as a source of them, the Bible serving the purposes of his disorder better than most others. For the schizophrenic, a little ingenuity suffices: everything fits. Like a man in a lighted house looking "out" a window at night, he sees only the reflection of what's inside. Then all zeal becomes dangerous, all thought deranged, all hope delusion, grief despair, and fear, instead of being the beginning of wisdom, becomes paranoia. This is the situation described by Richard as being caused by a lack of the discernment, or discretion, which is symbolized in the story by the late-born Joseph. For Richard, as for Jesus Ben-Sirach,[6] making the right decision boils down to taking the right advice and making it one's own; but with breathtaking good sense he points out that we aren't usually ready to receive good advice, even if we do get it, unless prepared by long and disappointing experience rightly understood. Only then can we "do according to counsel what we are stirred to do by inward promptings." The soul's long preparation is traced in the symbolism of the brothers born before Joseph.

For us to see out the night window we have to quench the lights inside, which is to say, mortify the ego, accept the grief we feel at its loss, and then receive the comfort of hope that leads to the inward sensation of God's

---

5. Augustine's *Confessions*, bk. 8, ch. 12. A good book on typology -- the study of prefiguration and postfiguration -- is A.C. Charity's *Events and Their Afterlife* (Cambridge, England, 1966).

6. Eccles. 32.24.

love and a nascent joy of praise -- these are Reuben, Simeon, Levi and Judah, meaning fear, grief, hope, and love, the first four sons of Leah, who stands for the affection or will. These virtues, Richard says, are sufficient for salvation but not for perfection. Going farther on our spiritual path we approach meditation by learning to still the inward jabbering of our imagination -- she is Bilhah, Rachel's handmaid -- and when we succeed in that we may begin to have visions that give us a palpable foretaste of hell and heaven -- those visions are Bilhah's sons, Dan and Naphtali. I don't believe these are just things a preacher might invent to coerce or entice obedience, though I doubt Richard would disapprove of such a use; I think rather of the visions of Dame Julian of Norwich or of those described in the Tibetan Book of the Dead. By them we are inwardly sobered and strengthened, so that we spontaneously exercise abstinence and patience -- Zilpah's two, Gad and Asher. After the imagination, the senses are brought under control. Zilpah stands for the senses. Then the affection or will, Leah, becomes fertile again and we experience a joyous inward sweetness along with a cleansed hatred of sin and an appropriate, Godgiven, sense of shame -- Issachar, Zebulun, and the one daughter, Dinah. Only after all that does Rachel give birth to Joseph, the favorite son, who is the discretion by which we are enabled to receive the truth when it comes to us. I find it somehow comforting, on my own quest, to have it confirmed that discretion -- what you'd think you'd have to have even to begin -- is the last stage of the soul before contemplation itself. The world moves on hasty judgments, but deep discernment is slow coming. You might have to wait.

Richard tells us that in a regular development it's a long time after the late coming of discretion that the soul finally goes outside its darkened house to experience contemplation. The family moves back to Canaan amidst difficulties and goes through all sorts of adventures before Rachel bears again, by the road to Bethlehem. And then, when Benjamin is born, she dies. She is reason, and she dies because in the ecstasy of contemplation we know even as we are known.[7] In a commentary on Psalm 113.4/114.4 Richard says that philosophers and theologians are correctly called speculatives because

---

7.     I Cor. 13.12.

they see the invisible things of God as if in a *speculum*, a mirror, and darkly. But it's given to the contemplative to see face to face. "Contemplating the revealed glory of God's face they see truth uncovered in its simplicity, without mirror or darkness." The contemplatives are the mountains that leap like rams, he says, and the speculatives the little hills that skip like young sheep.[8]

Richard's method of interpretation doesn't work without a cleansing of the soul and an abandonment of the ego's concerns -- humility -- and the kind of knowledge he aims for requires a passionate identification with its object -- charity. In fact, it would be hard to say whether we pursue knowledge so as to attain these virtues or exercise them so as to attain knowledge. It's a different kind of knowledge entirely from the kind that supposes alienation and promises control, according to which the knower is completely separate from what he knows and could know it without knowing himself. Our kind of knowledge shimmers back and forth. The self disappears, then you know yourself. Or, you realize that the God you kneel to and the enemy you despise are really you, some kind of projection: but at the very moment you deeply realize that they're you, you realize that they're Other than you, and you are free. Reading the Bible for such knowledge, you see that it implies everything it says everywhere, so that every part contains the unity of the whole. It lives the same way your dreams do, or any prophetic art; Blake said, "The Torso is as much a Unity as the Laocöon."[9] In a way it's true enough to say that Richard understands by reading into the Bible what he already knows. But I believe that's the kind of reading Jesus meant when he was talking about understanding his parables and warned us that "to them that have shall it be given and from them that have not shall it be taken away, even that little which they have."[10]

---

8.    *Adnotatio in Psalmum CXIII*, in Migne, *Patrologia Latina*, vol. 196, (Paris, 1880), cols. 335 ff. Translated in part by Clare Kirchberger in *Richard of Saint-Victor: Selected Writings on Contemplation* (London, 1957), p. 242.

9.    "On Homer's Poetry" in Erdman, ed., *The Poetry and Prose of William Blake* (New York, 1965), p. 267.

10.   Mark 4.25, Luke 8.18.

Maybe there was somebody named Jacob who had twelve sons and a daughter by his two wives and their handmaids, and maybe the wives said what the Bible says they did when the babies were born, so that the babies were named from what the wives had said -- that sort of thing gets remembered in some families. If so, it wouldn't keep those sons from being remembered centuries later as eponymous ancestors of the tribes who came out of Egypt. Jacob himself foresaw that they would when he gave his sons the oracular blessing recorded in the forty-ninth chapter of Genesis, just before he died: he was looking on into the future in terms of Abraham's covenant, and his sons were already starting to look like tribes to him. By Moses' time they had indeed become tribes (with the adjustment that Joseph's sons, Ephraim and Manassa, were separate tribes and the Levites were now a priestly caste not a tribe, the number remaining at twelve). Moses too blessed each tribe, just before his death on the plain below Pisgah, as is written at the end of Deuteronomy. This kind of layering keeps on building up in the tradition -- in the song of Deborah in Joshua, in what Jeremiah says about Rachel's children that Matthew quotes and reinterprets in his Gospel, and on down through the fathers to Richard and for that matter to Blake's *Jerusalem*.[11] Richard's own vision cuts back through these layers, following his master Hugh's emphasis on the literal level of interpretation, to the original personal family situation, with its disappointments, stubborn hopes, surprises, everyday conflicts, anger and humor, and he sees mirrored there the struggle of the soul for perfection. Looking at that, and at the etymologies of the names, he understands why the Psalm says "There is Benjamin a youth in ecstasy of mind."[12]

The idea that reason dies and falls away in the ecstasy of contemplation was hardly an unusual or surprising one, having always had the universal witness of experience, but it was being severely challenged in

---

[11.] Song of Deborah: Judges 5. Rachel: Jer. 31.15, Matt. 2.17-18. Blake's *Jerusalem*: e.g. pl. 16, ll. 28-67; Erdman, pp. 158-9.

[12.] Ps. 67.28 in the Douai Version, translating the Vulgate that follows the Septuagint and is quite different from the Authorized Version. This is the seed from which the whole idea of Richard's treatise springs: if Benjamin stands for contemplation then his brothers must stand for the states of the soul that lead up to it. See my note at the very end of the treatise, p. 48 below.

Richard's time. Abelard and his followers, excited over their new method of dialectic, were claiming that the intellect could search out everything, that in fact you couldn't even believe in what you didn't understand, that there isn't any truth that can't be rationally and precisely expressed -- wild things like that. They were intelligent, and good at controversy, and ambitious, and contemptuous of any thought not formulated according to their method. As often happens, these qualities endowed them with intellectual glamor and made them formidable in the academic politics of their day. They tended to infest the universities, where by their own lights they did good work. It isn't exactly true that they were unspiritual, just that to do what they were doing it wouldn't matter whether they were spiritual or not. They looked out for each other professionally, and they were dangerous in a fight. Abelard himself was indirectly responsible for the foundation of the abbey at St. Victor's, where Richard lived and wrote. It was founded by one of Abelard's former teachers, William of Champeaux, after Abelard had driven him away from the schools of Paris by savage argument and ridicule. William retired with a small community to a hermitage just outside the city wall, aiming to lead a quiet and holy life. (Or maybe he wanted to nurse his wounded vanity and ambition, as Abelard said.) But pupils followed him there, and he began teaching; the community grew and, just as William was leaving it to become a bishop, the hermitage was established as an abbey under the Rule of St. Augustine.

That it should be Augustine's rule is significant because Augustine was both mystic and theologian. From the beginning the aim of the Victorines was to avoid the overreaction of the Cistercians and Benedictines, who opposed the dialecticians with such rancor that they turned away in disgust, leaving theology pretty much in their hands. Mysticism came to seem incompatible with orderly thought, as it has seemed to many down to this day. You wouldn't guess from the writings of Hugh or Richard that there was any controversy, either between ecstasy and reason or between themselves and any others.[13] For them all knowledge of any kind is valuable,

---

13. A younger canon at St. Victor's, Walter, did write an angry attack on dialectic called *Against the Four Labyrinths of France*, the "labyrinths" being Abelard, Gilbert de la Porrée, Peter Lombard, and Peter of Poitiers.

and logic and speculation valid for their use. As I've already said (if on slight evidence from what we have before us)[14] the thrust of their Biblical study was to rescue the Letter from the trash bin where Gregory the Great had tossed it, insisting on the validity of historical knowledge as well as of moral or mystical interpretation. And their study of the letter was critical, too. Both Hugh and Richard consulted with Jewish scholars and learned some Hebrew, to get back freshly at the meaning.[15] To recognize the limitations of reason isn't necessarily to reject all knowledge and systematic thought.

Reason is the favorite wife, Rachel. Jacob has to work seven years to marry her, and after he is tricked into marrying the affection instead, Leah, he works seven years more and thinks them like a few days because his love for Rachel is so great. She is the mother of the favorite sons, and when she dies bringing forth contemplation she's mourned. Dante embodies the same truth in the figure of Virgil, who stands for something like reason. Virgil guides Dante through hell and climbs with him up Purgatory mountain; he's the one Dante turns to instinctively at the top when Beatrice, who stands for grace, is approaching: "Not a drop of blood in me but trembles: I know the signs of the old fire." When he sees that Virgil has disappeared Dante mourns for him as for his dear father, in whom he had entrusted himself for his salvation (until Beatrice tells him she'll really give him something to mourn about).[16] Reason isn't denied nor is our emotional attachment to it

---

[14] *Cf.* Beryl Smalley, *The Study of the Bible in the Middle Ages* (Oxford, 1952), ch.3.

[15] Apparently some of Richard's interpretations of Bible names are his own: I haven't found any other authority for the meanings he ascribes to Bilhah, Zilpah and Leah. Perhaps his knowledge of Hebrew explains why his quotations from the Bible are so often different from the Vulgate text -- that, and the fact that he no doubt often quoted from memory.

[16] *Pur.*, cto. 30. The direct intervention of grace, Beatrice, first chastens Dante, then becomes his guide up through the heavens until without regret she leaves him to another guide, St. Bernard of Clairvaux. I suppose Dante means we do go back to our books.

Abelard, who counted Bernard among his many enemies, is curiously absent from the *Comedy* where so many earthly enmities are reconciled. Perhaps he was still bent over carrying a boulder down on the terrace of Pride and Dante didn't see him when passing that way. Richard of St. Victor is among the philosophers in the sphere of the sun, but in naming him there Dante acknowledges his mysticism saying that he was "in contemplation more than man." (*Par.*, cto. 10, 11. 131-2)

considered evil. It's just that to enter the higher state of contemplation we have to extinguish the light of reason and be forsaken in the darkness, grief, and fright of unknowing.

No doubt it was the reasonable and systematic aspect of Richard's thought that made him accessible to the following centuries. As we have seen, his *Benjamin Minor* tells in an orderly way about the soul's approach to contemplation. His *Benjamin Major* is said to be the first systematic treatment of contemplation itself. Because it is systematic it leaves a stamp by which its influence can easily be traced: on Bonaventure and the Franciscans, on Dante (who used its mystical psychology when he laid out his *Paradiso*), on Ruysbroeck and Eckhardt, Walter Hilton and Rolle, on Bernardino de Laredo, whose *Ascent of Mount Sion* was the book Santa Teresa of Avila turned to in her own spiritual crisis, and on shoals of Spanish mystics down into the Seventeenth Century.[17] It was the stamp of system and the precision of Richard's definitions that led Ezra Pound to cite the *Benjamin Major* in a Confucianist essay on good government he wrote in Mussolini's Rome during the Second World War.[18] But what Richard was making accessible, what carried the system, was his witness of unknowable things.

Aside from the Bible Richard's principal written source for mystical thought, or for a way to talk about it, was Dionysius the Areopagite, who

---

17. Clare Kirchenberger traces Richard's influence in more detail in *Richard of St. Victor: Selected Writings on Contemplation* (London, 1957), pp. 57-74. On the Spanish mystics see E. Allison Peers' edition of Bernardino de Laredo's *Ascent of Mount Sion* (London, 1952), pp. 43-8, and *Studies of the Spanish Mystics* (3 vols., New York, 1951) *passim*. Fray Luís de Granada, Luís de Leon, Francisco de Osuna, Fray Juan de los Angeles, García de Cisneros, Tomás de Jesús, Juan Falconi, Jesus Maria Quíroga, Pérez de Valdivia, Jerónimo Plañes, Fray José Maldonado, Antonio Panes, Diego Alvarez de Paz, Melchor de Villanueva, Nicolas de Arneya, and Juan Eusebio Nieremberg all show the trace of Richard's thought.

18. "A Visiting Card," in *Selected Prose 1909-1965*, ed. William Cookson (London, 1973), p. 303. Later, in St. Elizabeth's, Pound reread the two Benjamins; he copied out fourteen brief passages and made translations (Cookson, pp. 73-4). There is an allusion to Richard in Canto 90: the human soul is
>   Not love but that love flows from it
>   ex animo
>   & cannot ergo delight in itself
>   but only in the love flowing from it

everybody then believed was among the few hearers in Athens who didn't reject St. Paul when he preached on the hill there called the Areopagus.[19] Most people in Richard's day also believed he was the same St. Denis who was the apostle to the Gauls and patron saint of France, who, after he was beheaded in Paris in 272, got up and carried his head the six miles to the town where he would be buried, whence its name, St. Denis. Nobody knows who wrote the treatises ascribed to this Dionysius: the *Celestial Hierarchies*, the *Church Hierarchies*, the *Divine Names*, the *Mystical Theology*, and ten epistles. "A Syrian monk of the Fifth or Sixth Century" is close enough. He is said to have derived his teachings from Eastern Christianity (Gregory of Nyssa) and from Neoplatonism (Plotinus), and for all I know that's true. It's also true that he sounds a little like Chuang Tzu sometimes, or Huang Po, or the Heart Sutra. The *Mystical Theology* (or *Denis's Hid Divinity* as it's called in the Middle English Version almost certainly made by our same translator of the *Benjamin Minor*) takes the form of instructions on the mystical life of the spirit offered to one of St. Paul's other companions, Timothy. It begins with the advice that Timothy enter into divine apathia divine athambia divine aphasia:

> Forsake with a strong and wise and eager contrition both your bodily senses (as hearing, seeing, smelling, tasting, and touching), and also your spiritual perceptions, or the working of your understanding; and everything that could be known without by the five senses, or within by spiritual perceptions; and everything that is now, or has been though it be not now, and everything that is not now but may be in time to come, though it be not now...

Timothy is to forsake not only all that but also

> all divine lights and all heavenly sounds and words, and [he is to] enter with affection into darknes where truly he is, as the Scripture shows, who is above all.

An example from Scripture is Moses,[20]

---

[19]. Acts 17.33-4.
[20]. Exod. 34.

> who is solitude of affection departed from these chosen priests and entered alone into the darkness of unknowing, which darkness is truly hid; in which he sheds all knowable knowing; and nevertheless is made in an invisible and ungropable way to feel in experience the presence of him that is above all things, not sensing nor thinking of himself. But in emptying out all knowing that is of any thing that is not yet wholly unknown he is knit to him in the best way; and because he knows nothing he is made to be knowing above mind.

You might have a book like that on your shelf a long time without reading it unless you knew someone else to read it with. This is the apophatic theology of Eastern Christianity, the *via negativa*, and like Buddhist thought it does sound negative, life-denying, or plain silly to anyone who doesn't know how to apply it -- unless it sound too alluring by half, and be taken as excuse and authority for all kinds of genuine silliness, as can also happen. Richard was valuable -- is valuable -- both for his steady witness of the sublime darkness of contemplation and for the candor and good sense with which he approaches it.

The same can be said for his Middle English translator, who in addition to translating the *Benjamin* and the *Denis's Hid Divinity* probably wrote *The Cloud of Unknowing* and a handful of short pieces: *An Epistle of Prayer, An Epistle of Privy Counsel, An Epistle of Discretion in the Stirrings of the Soul*, and *A Treatise of Discretion of Spirits*. His mind is a little more stark than Richard's. His version of the *Benjamin Minor* strips Richard's treatise down with casual authority, leaving out much that is beautiful (in the way of allegory or luxuriation of Scripture) and quite a bit that is intellectually worthy (in the way of theory of perception and psychology). What he aims at always is the practical achievement of contemplative prayer. So he not only takes things away but adds others, for instance the advice near the end about praying the name of Jesus. In *An Epistle of Prayer* he has another idea: if you really want to rule your heart while praying, begin by convincing yourself that you will surely die when your prayer is ended, or even before. That will help your concentration. And in him this being so stark, and so totally purposeful, goes with great charm and a complete lack of grimness or sanctimony. Like Richard he has a deep enthusiasm for the life of the spirit, the kind of faith that embraces difficulties with all eagerness, an athletic kind of love. His charm is the charm of subtle plainness, like Chaucer's or Dame Julian's; in his humor and forbearance he is like Chaucer again, or like the author of the *Ancrene Riwle*; in his freshness and sincerity he is like the English Franciscans who were writing religious lyrics during his time or a little after. From a literary point of view this unaffected and plain-looking subtlety is the sublime English quality in devotional writing, something that resurfaces later on in Herbert and Vaughan. By comparison the Italian religious lyrics of the time seem ingenious, and even the great Spanish mystics seem baroque and ornate: wonderful, but ingenious, and baroque and ornate. I don't want to make invidious comparisons, just to describe the best I can what the flavor is. St. Paul said that great eloquence becomes like a tinkling gong or rattling cymbal if it has not charity. This writer shows what great plainness is like when that same charity makes it incandescent.

# OLD TESTAMENT READINGS ON THE TWELVE PATRIARCHS

# OLD TESTAMENT READINGS ON THE TWELVE PATRIARCHS

The text is from the Douai Version which is mainly a translation of the Vulgate and so represents the version most familiar to medieval readers (though Richard's quotations often differ from it considerably). When necessary the spelling of names is changed to conform with that of the Authorized version.

## I. THE BIRTHS OF JACOB'S CHILDREN

GENESIS 29. 1-35, 30. 1-25:
*Eleven sons and a daughter are born to Jacob while he is living with Laban.*

### CHAPTER 29

1. Then Jacob went on in his journey, and came into the east country.
2. And he saw a well in the field, and three flocks of sheep lying by it; for the beasts were watered out of it, and the mouth thereof was closed with a great stone.
3. And the custom was, when all the sheep were gathered together, to roll away the stone, and after the sheep were watered, to put it on the mouth of the well again.
4. And he said to the shepherds: Brethren, whence are you? They answered: Of Haran.
5. And he asked them, saying: Know you Laban the son of Nahor? They said: We know him.
6. He said: Is he in health? He is in health, say they: and behold Rachel his daughter cometh with his flock.
7. And Jacob said: There is yet much day remaining, neither is it time to bring the flocks into the folds again. First give the sheep drink, and so lead them back to feed.
8. They answered: We cannot, till all the cattle be gathered together, and we remove the stone from the well's mouth, that we may water the flocks.

9. They were yet speaking, and behold Rachel came with her father's sheep: for she fed the flock.

10. And when Jacob saw her, and knew her to be his cousin-german, and that they were the sheep of Laban, his uncle: he removed the stone wherewith the well was closed.

11. And having watered the flock, he kissed her: and lifting up his voice, wept.

12. And he told her that he was her father's brother, and the son of Rebecca. But she went in haste and told her father,

13. Who, when he heard that Jacob his sister's son was come, ran forth to meet him; and embracing him, and heartily kissing him, brought him into his house. And when he had heard the causes of his journey,

14. He answered: Thou art my bone and my flesh. And after the days of one month were expired,

15. He said to him: Because thou art my brother, shalt thou serve me without wages? Tell me what wages thou wilt have.

16. Now he had two daughters, the name of the elder was Leah: and the younger was called Rachel.

17. But Leah was blear eyed: Rachel was well favoured, and of a beautiful countenance.

18. And Jacob being in love with her, said: I will serve thee seven years for Rachel thy younger daughter.

19. Laban answered: It is better that I give her to thee than to another man; stay with me.

20. So Jacob served seven years for Rachel: and they seemed but a few days, because of the greatness of his love.

21. And he said to Laban: Give me my wife; for now the time is fulfilled, that I may go in unto her.

22. And he, having invited a great number of his friends to the feast, made the marriage.

23. And at night he brought in Leah, his daughter, to him,

24. Giving his daughter a handmaid, named Zilpah. Now when Jacob had gone in to her according to custom, when morning was come he saw it was Leah:

25. And he said to his father-in-law: What is it that thou didst mean to do? Did not I serve thee for Rachel? Why hast thou deceived me?
26. Laban answered: It is not the custom in this place to give the younger in marriage first.
27. Make up the week of days of this match: and I will give thee her also, for the service that thou shalt render me other seven years.
28. He yielded to his pleasure: and after the week was past, he married Rachel,
29. To whom her father gave Bilhah for her servant.
30. And having at length obtained the marriage he wished for, he preferred the love of the latter before the former, and served with him other seven years.
31. And the Lord seeing that he despised Leah, opened her womb, but her sister remained barren.
32. And she conceived and bore a son, and called his name Reuben, saying: The Lord saw my affliction, Now my husband will love me.
33. And again she conceived and bore a son, and said: Because the Lord heard that I was despised, he hath given this also to me. And she called his name Simeon.
34. And she conceived the third time, and bore another son, and said: Now also my husband will be joined to me, because I have borne him three sons. And therefore she called his name Levi.
35. The fourth time she conceived and bore a son, and said: Now will I praise the Lord. And for this she called him Judah. And she left bearing.

## CHAPTER 30

1. And Rachel, seeing herself without children, envied her sister, and said to her husband: Give me children, otherwise I shall die.
2. And Jacob being angry with her, answered: Am I as God, who hath deprived thee of the fruit of thy womb?
3. But she said: I have here my servant Bilhah. Go in unto her, that she may bear upon my knees, and I may have children by her.
4. And she gave him Bilhah in marriage: who,
5. When her husband had gone in unto her, conceived and bore a son.

6. And Rachel said: The Lord hath judged for me, and hath heard my voice, giving me a son. And therefore she called his name Dan.

7. And again Bilhah conceived and bore another,

8. For whom Rachel said: God hath compared me with my sister, and I have prevailed. And she called him Naphtali.

9. Leah, perceiving that she had left off bearing, gave Zilpah her handmaid to her husband.

10. And when she had conceived and brought forth a son,

11. She said: Happily: and therefore called his name Gad.

12. Zilpah also bore another.

13. And Leah said: This is for my happiness: for women will call me blessed. Therefore she called him Asher.

14. And Reuben, going out in the time of the wheat harvest into the field, found mandrakes: which he brought to his mother Leah. And Rachel said: Give me part of thy son's mandrakes.

15. She answered: Dost thou think it a small matter, that thou hast taken my husband from me, unless thou take also my son's mandrakes? Rachel said: He shall sleep with thee this night, for thy son's mandrakes.

16. And when Jacob returned at even from the field, Leah went out to meet him, and said: Thou shalt come in unto me, because I have hired thee for my son's mandrakes. And he slept with her that night.

17. And God heard her prayer: and she conceived and bore the fifth son,

18. And said: God hath given me a reward, because I gave my handmaid to my husband. And she called his name Issachar.

19. And Leah conceived again, and bore the sixth son,

20. And said: God hath endowed me with a good dowry: this turn also my husband will be with me, because I have borne him six sons. And therefore she called his name Zebulun.

21. After whom she bore a daughter, named Dinah.

22. The Lord also remembering Rachel, heard her, and opened her womb,

23. And she conceived, and bore a son, saying: God hath taken away my reproach.

24. And she called his name Joseph, saying: The Lord give me also another son.

25. And when Joseph was born, Jacob said to his father-in-law: Send me away that I may return into my country, and to my land.

GENESIS 35. 9-26
*Much later, beside the highway to Bethlehem, Rachel gives birth to Benjamin and dies.*

## CHAPTER 35

9. And God appeared again to Jacob, after he returned from Mesopotamia of Syria, and he blessed him,

10. Saying: Thou shalt not be called any more Jacob, but Israel shall be thy name. And he called him Israel.

11. And said to him: I am God Almighty. Increase thou and be multiplied. Nations and peoples of nations shall be from thee, and kings shall come out of thy loins.

12. And the land which I gave to Abraham and Isaac, I will give to thee, and to thy seed after thee.

13. And he departed from him.

14. But he set up a monument of stone, in the place where God had spoken to him: pouring drink offerings upon it, and pouring oil thereon:

15. And calling the name of that place Bethel.

16. And going forth from thence, he came in the spring-time to the land which leadeth to Ephrata: wherein when Rachel was in travail,

17. By reason of her hard labour, she began to be in danger, and the midwife said to her: Fear not, for thou shalt have this son also.

18. And when her soul was departing for pain, and death was now at hand, she called the name of her son Benoni, that is, The son of my pain: but his father called him Benjamin, that is, The son of the right hand.

19. So Rachel died, and was buried in the highway that leadeth to Ephrata. This is Bethlehem.

20. And Jacob erected a pillar over her sepulchre. This is the pillar of Rachel's monument, to this day.

21. Departing thence, he pitched his tent beyond the Flock tower.

22.   And when he dwelt in that country, Reuben went, and slept with Bilhah, the concubine of his father: which he was not ignorant of. Now the sons of Jacob were twelve.

23.   The sons of Leah: Reuben the firstborn, and Simeon, and Levi, and Judah, and Issacar, and Zebulun.

24.   The sons of Rachel: Joseph and Benjamin.

25.   The sons of Bilhah, Rachel's handmaid: Dan and Naphtali.

26.   The sons of Zelpha, Leah's handmaid: Gad and Asher. These are the sons of Jacob, that were born to him in Mesopotamia of Syria.

## II. JACOB'S BLESSING

**GENESIS 49. 1-32**
*Before he dies in Egypt, Jacob pronounces a blessing on each of his twelve sons: "every one, with their proper blessings."*

### CHAPTER 49

1.   And Jacob called his sons, and said to them: Gather yourselves together that I may tell you the things that shall befall you in the last days.

2.   Gather yourselves together, and hear, O ye sons of Jacob: hearken to Israel your father.

3.   Reuben, my firstborn, thou art my strength, and the beginning of my sorrow: excelling in gifts, greater in command.

4.   Thou art poured out as water, grow thou not: because thou wentest up to thy father's bed, and didst defile his couch.

5.   Simeon and Levi brethren: vessels of iniquity, waging war.

6.   Let not my soul go into their counsel, nor my glory be in their assembly: because in their fury they slew a man, and in their self-will they undermined a wall.

7.   Cursed by their fury, because it was stubborn: and their wrath because it was cruel. I will divide them in Jacob, and will scatter them in Israel.

8.   Judah, thee shall thy brethren praise. Thy hands shall be on the necks of thy enemies: the sons of thy father shall bow down to thee.

9. Judah is a lion's whelp; to the prey, my son, thou art gone up. Resting thou hast couched as a lion, and as a lioness. Who shall rouse him?
10. The sceptre shall not be taken away from Judah, nor a ruler from his thigh, till he come that is to be sent: and he shall be the expectation of nations.
11. Tying his foal to the vineyard, and his ass, O my son, to the vine. He shall wash his robe in wine, and his garment in the blood of the grape.
12. His eyes are more beautiful than wine: and his teeth whiter than milk.
13. Zebulun shall dwell on the sea shore, and in the road of ships, reaching as far as Sidon.
14. Issachar shall be a strong ass lying down between the borders.
15. He saw rest that it was good: and the land that it was excellent. And he bowed his shoulder to carry, and became a servant under tribute.
16. Dan shall judge his people like another tribe in Israel.
17. Let Dan be a snake in the way, a serpent in the path, that biteth the horse's heels that his rider may fall backward.
18. I will look for thy salvation, O Lord.
19. Gad, being girded, shall fight before him: and he himself shall be girded backward.
20. Asher: his bread shall be fat and he shall yield dainties to kings.
21. Naphtali: a hart let loose, and giving words of beauty.
22. Joseph is a growing son, a growing son and comely to behold: the daughters run to and fro upon the wall.
23. But they that held darts provoked him, and quarrelled with him, and envied him.
24. His bow rested upon the strong, and the bands of his arms and his hands were loosed, by the hands of the mighty one of Jacob: thence he came forth a pastor, the stone of Israel.
25. The God of thy father shall be thy helper, and the Almighty shall bless thee with the blessing of the deep that lieth beneath, with the blessing of the breasts and of the womb.
26. The blessings of thy father are strengthened with the blessings of his father: until the desire of the everlasting hills should come. May they be

upon the head of Joseph, and upon the crown of the Nazarite among his brethren.

27. Benjamin a ravenous wolf, in the morning shall eat the prey, and in the evening shall divide the spoil.

28. All these are the twelve tribes of Israel: these things their father spoke to them, and he blessed every one, with their proper blessings.

29. And he charged them, saying: I am now going to be gathered to my people: bury me with my fathers in the double cave, which is in the field of Ephron the Hethite,

30. Over against Mambre in the land of Canaan, which Abraham bought together with the field of Ephron the Hethite for a possession to bury in.

31. There they buried him, and Sarah his wife. There was Isaac buried with Rebecca his wife. There also Leah doth lie buried.

32. And when he had ended the commandments, wherewith he instructed his sons, he drew up his feet upon the bed, and died. And he was gathered to his people.

### III. MOSES' BLESSING

DEUTERONOMY 33. 1-29
*As death approaches him on the plains of Moab, Moses blesses the twelve tribes.*

### CHAPTER 33

1. This is the blessing, where the man of God Moses blessed the children of Israel, before his death.

2. And he said: The Lord came from Sinai, and from Seir he rose up to us. He hath appeared from mount Pharan, and with him thousands of saints. In his right hand a fiery law.

3. He hath loved the people: all the saints are in his hand. And they that approach to his feet, shall receive of his doctrine.

4. Moses commanded us a law, the inheritance of the multitude of Jacob.

5. He shall be king with the most right: the princes of the people being assembled with the tribes of Israel.

6. Let Reuben live, and not die: and be he small in number.

7. This is the blessing of Judah: Hear, O Lord, the voice of Judah, and bring him in unto his people. His hands shall fight for him, and he shall be his helper against his enemies.
8. To Levi also he said: Thy perfection, and thy doctrine be to thy holy man, whom thou hast proved in the temptation, and judged at the waters of contradiction.
9. Who hath said to his father, and to his mother: I do not know you, and to his bretheren: I know you not: and their own children they have not known. These have kept thy word, and observed thy covenant.
10. Thy judgments, O Jacob, and thy law, O Israel: they shall put incense in thy wrath and holocaust upon thy altar.
11. Bless, O Lord, his strength and receive the works of his hands. Strike the backs of his enemies, and let not them that hate him rise.
12. And to Benjamin he said: The best beloved of the Lord shall dwell confidently in him. As in a bride chamber shall he abide all the day long: and between his shoulders shall be rest.
13. To Joseph also he said: Of the blessing of the Lord he his land, of the fruits of heaven, and of the dew, and of the deep that lieth beneath:
14. Of the fruits brought forth by the sun and by the moon:
15. Of the tops of the ancient mountains, of the fruits of the everlasting hills:
16. And of the fruits of the earth, and of the fulness thereof. The blessings of him that appeared in the bush, come upon the head of Joseph, and upon the crown of the Nazarite among his brethren.
17. His beauty as of the firstling of a bullock, his horns as the horns of a rhinoceros: with them shall he push the nations even to the ends of the earth. These are the multitudes of Ephraim; and these the thousands of Manasses.
18. And to Zebulun he said: Rejoice, O Zebulun, in thy going out: and Issachar in thy tabernacles.
19. They shall call the people to the mountain: there shall they sacrifice the victims of justice. Who shall suck as milk the abundance of the sea, and the hidden treasures of the sands.

20. And to Gad he said: Blessed be Gad in his breadth: he hath rested as a lion, and hath seized upon the arm and the top of the head.

21. And he saw his pre-eminence, that in his portion the teacher was laid up: who was with the princes of the people: and did the justices of the Lord, and his judgment with Israel.

22. To Dan also he said: Dan is a young lion: he shall flow plentifully from Bashan.

23. And to Naphtali he said: Naphtali shall enjoy abundance, and shall be full of the blessings of the Lord. He shall possess the sea and the south.

24. To Asher also he said: Let Asher be blessed with children, let him be acceptable to his brethren, and let him dip his foot in oil.

25. His shoes shall be iron and brass. As the days of thy youth, so also shall thy old age be.

26. There is no other God like the God of the rightest: he that is mounted upon the heaven is thy helper. By his magnificence the clouds run hither and thither.

27. His dwelling is above, and underneath, are the everlasting arms. He shall cast out the enemy from before thee, and shall say: Be thou brought to nought.

28. Israel shall dwell in safety, and alone. The eye of Jacob is a land of corn and wine, and the heavens shall be misty with dew.

29. Blessed art thou, Israel: Who is like to thee, O people, that art saved by the Lord? The shield of thy help, and the sword of thy glory. Thy enemies shall deny thee, and thou shalt tread upon their necks.

# A TREATISE OF THE STUDY OF WISDOM THAT MEN CALL BENJAMIN

## A TREATISE OF THE STUDY OF WISDOM THAT MEN CALL BENJAMIN

A great scholar named Richard of Saint Victor, in his book on the spiritual discipline that leads to mystical contemplation, witnesses and declares that God, whose gift is every good thing, has endowed man's soul with two faculties: one of them is reason and the other affection or will. Through reason we know, and through affection we experience or love. From reason spring right counsel and spiritual perception, and from affection spiritual desire and well-ordered feeling. And just as Rachel and Leah were both wives of Jacob, man's soul is married to God through the light of knowledge in the reason and sweetness of love in the affection. Jacob is understood as God, Rachel as reason, and Leah as affection.

Each of these wives took a handmaid: Rachel took Bilhah and Leah took Zilpah. Bilhah was a jabbermouth and Zilpah always drunk and always thirsty.[1] By Bilhah we understand imagination, which is servant to reason as Bilhah was to Rachel. By Zilpah we understand sensation, which is servant to affection as Zilpah was to Leah. And these ladies need their handmaids: so much so that without their handmaids all this world would do them no

---

1. These characterizations come not from the Biblical narrative but from folk etymologies on the names. *Cf. Benjamin Minor*, ch. 6: "So, because no matter how much she drinks she always has her mouth open to drink more, she's rightly called Zilpah, that is, *gaping mouth*....So in any case decrepit old men and inveterate old women have the habit of talking away without any listener, as if someone were there to take part in their conversation. Therefore she deserves to be called Bilhah, that is, *inveterate*, who imitates the habits of the elderly (Quia ergo quantumcunque bibat, semper ad bibendum inhiat, recte Zelpha, hoc est, *os inhians*, vocatur....Sic utique decrepiti senes, vel inveteratae anus, solent quaelibet absque omni auditore referre, et quasi aliquibus praesentibus cum eis sermonum conferre. Unde non immerito Bala, hoc est *inveterata*, dicitur, quae inveteratorum morem imitatur)." He may have learned these etymologies from Jewish scholars he knew and consulted. *Cf.* Beryl Smalley, *The Study of the Bible in the Middle Ages* (Oxford, 1956), p. 110. Modern "scientific" etymology has little to offer. According to the *Interpreter's Dictionary of the Bible (s. nn.)*, Bilhah probably means simplicity, modesty, or perhaps unconcern, and Zilpah "perhaps short-nosed."

good. Because without imagination reason can't know any of the outward physical things of creation, nor affection feel them without the senses.

And yet imagination jabbers on so impetuously in the mind's ear that in spite of anything her lady reason may do she won't be stilled. That's why often when we wish to pray so many different kinds of fantasies from unspiritual thoughts are running in our minds that we aren't able to drive them away no matter how hard we try. And that proves that Bilhah is a natural jabbermouth. The senses, too, are always so thirsty that all their lady affection may experience won't slake their thirst. The drink they desire is the enjoyment of fleshly, natural and worldly pleasures, for which the more she drinks the thirstier she gets. Because to fill up the appetite of the senses the whole world wouldn't suffice. And so it is that often when we think about God and spiritual things we would like to feel sweetness of love in our affection, and yet we can't, because we are so distracted by the eagerness of our senses. They are always greedily begging, and we have a fleshly compassion for them. And that proves that Zilpah is always thirsty and always drunk.

Just as Leah conceived by Jacob and bore seven children, and Zilpah conceived by Jacob and bore two children, and Bilhah conceived by Jacob and bore two children, and Rachel conceived by Jacob and bore two children: so affection conceives by the grace of God and brings forth seven virtues; and the senses conceive by the grace of God and bring forth two virtues; and the imagination conceives by the grace of God and brings forth two beholdings, or virtues; and reason conceives by the grace of God and brings forth two virtues. And the names of the children and of their virtues are shown in the figure below.

This figure shows the relationship of Jacob, his wives, their handmaids, and all their children. Next will be shown how the children were begotten, and in what order, and first, why it was Leah who first conceived.

The sons of Jacob by Leah mean nothing else but well-ordered affections or feelings in a man's soul: for if they weren't well-ordered they wouldn't be his. So the seven children of Leah are seven virtues, because virtue is nothing else but orderly and measured feeling in a man's soul. A man's feeling in his soul is well-ordered when it comes from the thing it

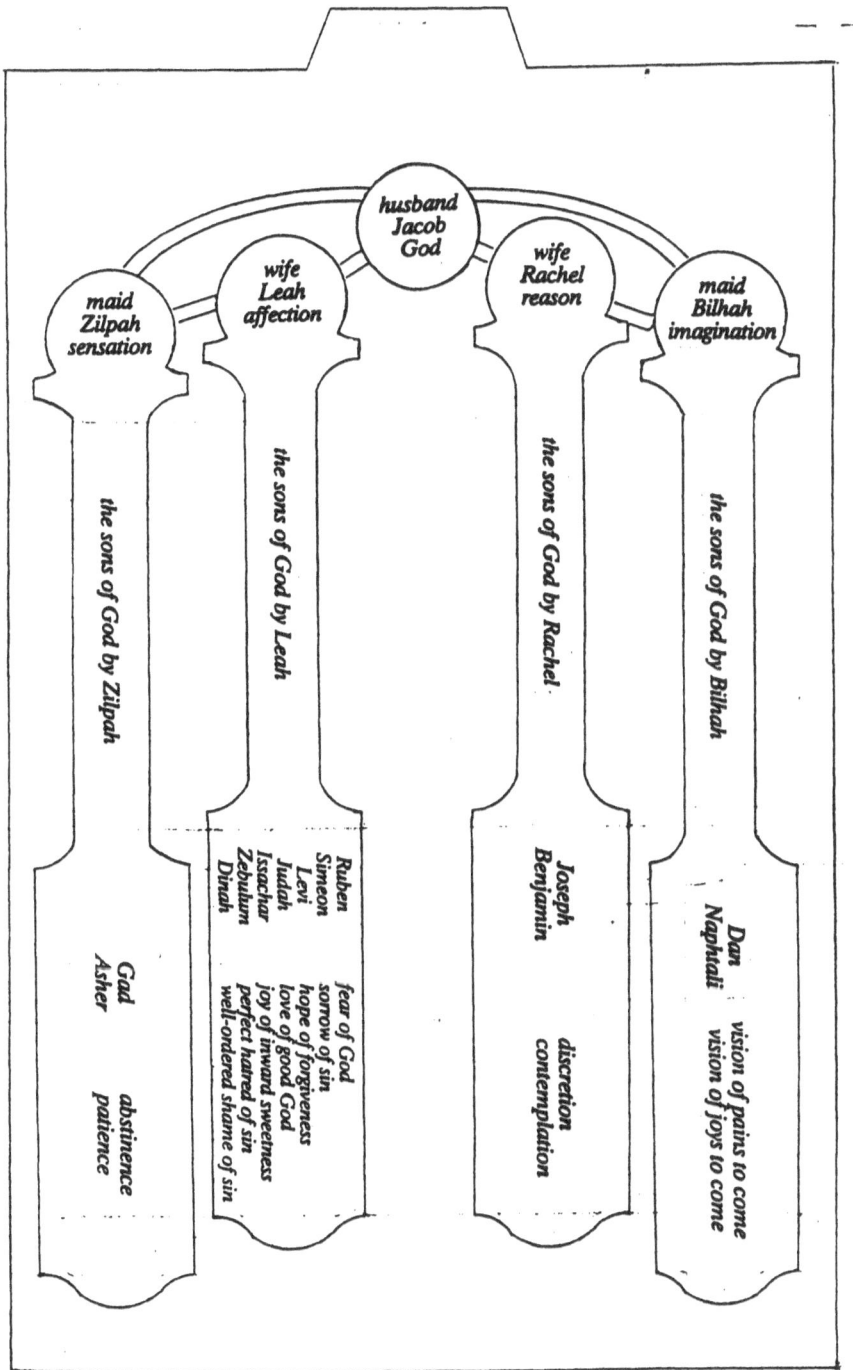

should come from. It is measured when it is as strong as it should be. These feelings in a man's soul can be now well-ordered and measured, and now disorderly and unmeasured. But when they are well-ordered and measured they can be considered sons of Jacob.

### + HOW THE VIRTUE FEAR ARISES IN THE AFFECTION +

The first child that Leah conceived by Jacob was Reuben, which means fear.[2] That's why the Psalm says, "The beginning of wisdom is fear of our Lord God."[3] This is the first virtue experienced in a man's affection, and without it man can have no other. So whoever wishes to bear such a son

---

[2.] The folk etymology for Reuben is embedded in the Biblical text, "son of sight" or "behold, a son." Richard quotes the former. But since in Richard's allegory Reuben is the beginning of wisdom his name must also mean "fear," according to the Psalm. This apparent confusion of the two ideas, seeing and fearing, opens onto a profound insight about the way we perceive, because when we fear we do see more vividly than otherwise. That dog on the beach in the Proteus episode of Joyce's *Ulysses* is so minutely observed and palpably expressed as it is because Joyce (and hence Stephen) was afraid of dogs. An experiment that Bertram Joseph performed about creating images in the mind of an audience illustrates the point even more clearly. As he tells it, he was lecturing with a troupe of English Method actors in a village school where no one knew the story of *Macbeth*. He had an actor recite twice the speech in which Banquo describes Macbeth's castle at Inverness to King Duncan. The first time the actor was to imagine that he was actually seeing what he described and to convey that image to the children as best as he could. But the children didn't see anything. Then Joseph took the actor aside and coached him to imagine Banquo's unspoken thoughts: about Macbeth's reaction to the witches and his premonitory shudder of guilt later when he heard that their prophecy was beginning to come true; about what might happen to make it come true; about Macbeth hurrying ahead, and waiting for them at Inverness. The actor was to concentrate on Banquo's *fears*, in a word, though the students didn't know anything about them.

> This guest of summer,
> The temple-haunting martlet, does approve,
> By his loved mansionry, that the heaven's breath
> Smells wooingly phere: no jutty, frieze,
> Buttress, nor coign of vantage, but this bird
> Hath made his pendent bed, and procreant cradle;
> Where they most bred and haunt, I have observ'd
> The air is delicate.   (I, vi, 3-11.)

This time when the actor said the words the students saw the castle.

[3.] Psalm 110.10 in the Vulgate and the Douai version; 111.10 in the Authorized Version and the Psalter. All subsequent references to the Psalms will cite both sources in that order. *Cf.* also Ps. 24.12-14/25.11-13, Prov. 1.7, 9.10, Eccles. 1.16.

must eagerly and often behold the evil things he has done. On one side he should think of the gravity of his offense, and, on the other side, of the power of his judge. Out of such a meditation comes fear, that's to say he does, Reuben, who is justly called *the son of sight*. Because anyone who can't envision torments to come and is not afraid to sin is really blind. And Reuben is well called *the son of sight* because when he was born his mother cried out "God has seen my humiliation."[4] And man's soul, in meditating on his old sin and the power of his judge, begins truly to discern God by feeling fear and also to be seen by God who looks back at him with pity.[5]

### + HOW GRIEF ARISES IN THE AFFECTION +

While Reuben is growing, Simeon is born, for after fear comes an urgent need for grief; because the more a man fears the punishment he has deserved the more bitterly he grieves at the sin he has done. At Simeon's birth Leah's cry was "Our Lord has heard that I am despised." That's why Simeon is called *hearing*; for when a man in bitter grief despises his old sins is when God begins to hear him, and the man also hears this blessed saying from God's own mouth: "Blessed are they who grieve, for they will be comforted."[6] Because in the hour that a sinner feels grief and turns away from his sin he will be saved. Holy Scripture testifies as much.[7] By Reuben

---

4. Gen. 29.32. Assuming that the reader will be familiar with Genesis twenty-nine and thirty (included above in "Old Testament Readings on the Twelve Patriarchs"), I shall not make any more footnote references to these two chapters.

5. The Middle English is "and also to be seen of God by rewarding of pite," translating closely the Latin "videri a Deo per respectum pietatis." "Pite" could be pity or piety or mercy.

    I suppose abstract theology would tell us that God sees everything, us included, all the time, so the idea that we "begin" to be seen by God is absurd. But in mystical psychology the idea of perception being reciprocal, and having a history, agrees with experience. The pity is the reflex of the holy fear, and like it intensifies perception; the eyebeam of that perception crosses, creating the sensation of being perceived.

6. Matt. 5.5.

7. Hodgson cites Ezech. 33.14-15, or 18.27. I should suggest Ps. 29.8b-12/30.8-12, "Thou turnedst away thy face from me: and I become troubled... Thou hast turned for me my mourning into joy" -- unless indeed Richard was already thinking of Psalm 50/51, which he soon quotes.

he is made meek, and by Simeon contrite, and he is punctured so he weeps. But as David witnesses in the Psalm, "a broken and contrite heart, O God, you will not despise."[8] And without doubt that kind of grief is what brings in true comfort.

### + HOW HOPE ARISES IN THE AFFECTION +

But I ask you what comfort can there be for them who truly fear God and bitterly grieve over their old sins, unless it be a true hope of forgiveness? -- which is the third son of Jacob. That is Levi, who is called *adding to* in the story. Because when the other two children, fear and grief, are given by God to a man's soul, there is no doubt that he, this third child who is hope, will follow without delay: he will be added to them, as the story tells of Levi. After his two brothers, Reuben and Simeon, had been given to their mother Leah, he, this Levi, was added to them. Pay attention to these words, that he was added, not given. And therefore it's said that man shall not presume to hope for forgiveness before the time his heart is humbled by fear and made contrite by grief. Without these two, hope is presumption; and where these two are, hope is added.

And so after grief comfort comes soon, as David says in the Psalm, "According to the multitude of griefs in my heart, your comforts have given joy to my soul."[9] That's why the Holy Ghost is called the Paraclete, that is, the Comforter, because he often comes down to comfort a soul in grief.

### + HOW LOVE ARISES IN THE AFFECTION +

And now a certain homeliness with God begins growing in a man's soul, and a kindling of love; so that often he feels not only visited by God, but greatly comforted by his coming. This homeliness and this kindling of love were what Leah felt with great joy when she cried, "Now shall my husband be coupled to me." The true spouse of our soul is God; and we are truly coupled

---

8.  Ps. 50.19/51.18.

9.  Ps. 93.19/94.19.

to him when we draw near him in hope and steady love. And as love comes after hope, so after Levi Judah was born, Leah's fourth son.

At his birth Leah cried out, "Now shall I confess praise to our Lord."[10] And therefore in the story Judah is called *praise*. In this degree of love man's soul offers praise clearly to God, and says with Leah "Now shall I confess praise to our Lord." Because until this feeling of love enters a man's soul, all that he does is done more out of fear than out of love. But in this state a man's soul both knows and feels God to be so sweet, so merciful, so good, so courtly, so true, so kind, so steady, so loving, and so homely that nothing remains in a man -- strength, knowledge, nor will -- that he doesn't offer it absolutely, freely, and intimately to God. This confession of praise comes not just from man's sinfulness but from God's goodness. And it's an important sign of a man's love when he is able to say freely to God that God is good. David speaks of this kind of praise often in the Psalms when he says "Make it known to God, for he is good."[11]

And now we have spoken of four of Leah's sons. After them, for a time, she left off childbearing. And a man's soul does suppose itself to be satisfied when it can feel its own love for true goodness. In fact this love is sufficient for our salvation, -- but not for our perfection. Because it comes to

---

10. Our English makes a distinction between confession and praise that neither the Latin nor the Middle English (nor indeed the Hebrew, I'm told) admits. "Modo confitebor Domino" says the Bible as Richard quotes it, and our Middle English author translates "Now schal I schrive to oure Lorde." The same word means both to reveal your own innerness, shameful as it may be, and to praise God for his goodness. There is a psychological truth in what our present language makes sound like a confusion. For it's true that we wouldn't presume to inform God of his own goodness -- that is, we would be unable to praise -- unless we experienced the "homeliness," as our author calls it, the sense of intimacy we can have only if we reveal ourselves. When our pride and secret shame thaw, we are released, and praise comes unbidden.

I believe this movement of feeling is written into the Mass at the Sursum Corda. "Lift up your miserable rotten and broken hearts." "We lift them as an offering, not because they're good, which they aren't, but because they are all we have." "If we can do that let us give thanks unto our Lord God." "It is right to give him thanks -- and praise."

11. Ps. 105.1/106.1, "Give glory to the Lord, for he is good." *Cf.* also 33.2/34.1, 107.3/108.2.

a perfect soul not only to be inflamed with ardent love in the affection, but also to be enlightened with the light of knowledge in the reason.

### + HOW THE DOUBLE SIGHT OF PAIN AND JOY ARISES IN THE IMAGINATION +

So when Judah is born -- that's to say, when love and desire for the good that is unseen and true are rising and growing in a man's affection -- is when Rachel covets childbirth -- that's to say, reason longs to know those things that the affection feels. For as it belongs to Leah, the affection, to love, so it belongs to Rachel, the reason, to know. From Leah, affection, spring measured and well-ordered feelings; and from Rachel, from reason, spring right knowing and clear understanding. And the more Judah grows, that's to say, love, the more Rachel desires to bear children: reason is eager to know.

But who is there who doesn't know how hard it is, and next to impossible, for a fleshly soul, ignorant in spiritual disciplines, to rise into the knowledge of invisible things and set the eye of contemplation on spiritual things? Because an ignorant and fleshly soul knows only bodily things, and nothing comes to the mind that couldn't be seen. And just the same the soul looks inward the best it can, and what it can't yet see clearly, by spiritual knowledge, it thinks about, by imagination. This is why Rachel had children by her handmaid before she could bear any herself. And so it is that, even though a man's soul may not yet get the light of spiritual knowledge in its reason, it already thinks it sweet to hold the mind on God and spiritual things in the imagination. As we understand by Rachel, reason, so her handmaid, Bilhah, is imagination. And so reason teaches us that it is more profitable to think about spiritual things by any means at all, yes, even if it be the kindling of our desire with mere pleasant fantasies, than it is to concern ourselves with the empty and lying things of this world. And therefore Bilhah gave birth to these two, Dan and Naphtali. Dan is to say the vision of future pain, and Naphtali the vision of future joy.

These two children are quite necessary, and also quite helpful to a soul at work, the one to put down all promptings of sin, and the other to rear up our will to good actions and to the kindling of our desire. Dan puts down the evil promptings of sin by the vision of future pain, and his brother, Naphtali, arouses our will to good actions and kindles holy desires by the vision of future joy. And therefore holy men, when stirred by any vile or unruly thoughts, set their minds on pains to come and so quench their temptation right at the start, before it can take the form of any vile delight in their soul. And whenever their devotion fails, and their pleasure in God and spiritual things gets cold (as often happens in this life because of the corruption of the flesh and for other reasons), they set their mind on the joy that is to come. And so they kindle their holy desires, and destroy their temptation in the beginning, before it come to any weariness or heaviness of sloth.

And because with Dan we condemn all unruly thoughts, he is well called *judgment* in the story. So his father, Jacob, said of him, "Dan shall judge his people."[12] And the story also tells that when Bilhah gave birth to Dan, Rachel said "Our Lord has judged me," by which she meant "Our Lord has got me even with my sister Leah." So reason, when she has received a vision of future torments, says that our Lord has got her even with her sister, affection. And Rachel said it because she could visualize in her imagination what had already made Leah feel fear and grief.

Then comes Naphtali, which is to say the vision of joy to come. At his birth Rachel said, "I am made like my sister Leah." That's why Naphtali is called *likeness* in the story. Thus reason says that she is like her sister affection, because where the affection had hope and love of future joy in her feeling, reason had got the vision of future joy in her imagination. Jacob said of Naphtali that he was a hind let loose saying words of beauty.[13] So, when we imagine the joys of heaven, we say that it is beautiful. Because Naphtali kindles holy desires wonderfully in our souls whenever we imagine the exaltation and the beauty of the joy in heaven.

---

12.    Gen. 49.16.

13.    Gen. 49.21.

## + HOW THE VIRTUES OF ABSTINENCE AND PATIENCE ARISE IN THE SENSES +

When Leah saw what joy her sister Rachel felt because of these two bastards born to the maid Bilhah, she called her own maid, Zilpah, to put to her husband so that she could feel joy along with her sister because of the two other bastards got from Zilpah. And that's the way a man's soul should be: when from time to time his reason has held back the eternal talkativeness of the imagination, and has put her under obedience to God, so that imagination becomes fecund helping reason to know, the affection should likewise hold in the lust and thirst of the senses and make them be obedient to God too, so that they bear their own fruit by helping her to feel.

But what fruit can sense bear, unless it be to learn to live temperately in easy things and patiently in hardships? These are the children of Zilpah, Gad and Asher. Gad is abstinence, and Asher is patience. Gad is born sooner and Asher later, because we must first learn inward discipline by astute abstinence and after that bear outward hardships by the strength of patience. Zilpah had painful childbirth, because abstinence and patience punish the senses sorely in the flesh. But what is pain to the senses becomes joy and bliss to the affection or will. That's why Gad is called *luck* in the story, or *blessedness*, whichever you want. So it's well said that abstinence in the senses is blessedness in the will. Because the less the senses are moved to delight by their pleasures, the more sweetness affection feels in her love. And later when Asher was born Leah said, "This will be for my joy." Because of that Asher is called *joyousness* in the story. And so it's well said that patient suffering in the senses is joy in the affection. Because the more hardship sensuality bears the more joyous the soul is in the affection.

And by abstinence and patience we shall understand not only moderation in food and drink, and endurance in outward tribulations, but in all kinds of fleshly, and natural, and worldly delights, and in all kinds of suffering, of body or spirit, inward or outward, reasonable or unreasonable, that through any of our five senses torment or delight the sensuality. In this way what the sensuality gives birth to helps her lady affection. There is great peace and rest in the soul that is neither drowned in the pleasures of sensuality nor troubled by its distress. Freedom from pleasure is won by Gad, and from pain by Asher.

Notice that Rachel's maid was sent in to the husband before Leah's was. And here's why: it's a fact that unless the jabbering of the imagination, which is to say the inrunning of idle thoughts, be first held back, the appetites of sensuality can't be controlled. So whoever wishes to abstain from fleshly and worldly pleasures must seldom or never think any idle thoughts. And therefore no man in this life will be able to despise perfectly the ease of the flesh, and to be unafraid of its distress, unless he first vividly imagine the rewards and torments that are to come.

Here we should learn how these four sons of the two servants wonderfully keep the citadel of our conscience from all temptations. Because any temptation arises either inwardly, by thought, or outwardly, by some of our five senses. But inside us Dan judges and condemns evil thoughts by visualization of pain, and Gad repels false delights from outside by use of abstinence. Dan is on watch inside, and Gad outside. The other two brothers help: Naphtali makes inward peace with Dan, and Asher strengthens Gad against panic. Dan terrifies the heart with horribility of hell, and Naphtali gladdens it with the promise of heavenly bliss. Asher helps Gad defend the city wall, and between them it isn't broken. Gad keeps ease from getting in, and Asher goes out to attack distress, an enemy he soon destroys by reminding conscience of his father's patience[14] and his brother Naphtali's promise; often, in fact, the more enemies he has the more material there is for his triumph. So when he has vanquished his own enemies, the adversities of this world, he turns on Gad's enemies to help destroy them. And without fail, whenever he joins in, they turn their backs

---

14.  Here I choose to ignore Hodgson's emendation, which is the only one she makes without any manuscript support. The best manuscripts read "the pacyence of his fader," which she emends to "the pacience of his parte" because, as she points out, the Latin goes "Sed Aser hosti suo facile illudit, dum partem tuetur, alta patientiae rupe munitam conspicit": our translator or an earlier scribe must have read "partem," part, as "patrem," father. But the Middle English isn't a close version of the Latin anyway (Grover Zinn translates the Latin "But Asher easily makes sport of his enemy; while he gazes at a part, he sees from the lofty rock of patience the fortified place that he defends"). I prefer to retain the sense our Middle English author made of it.

and run. The enemies of Gad are the flesh's delights. But truly, when a man starts to have patience enduring the pain of abstinence, false delight can find no place to lodge in him.

### + HOW THE JOY OF INWARD SWEETNESS ARISES IN THE AFFECTION +

When the enemies run away and the city is pacified is when a man finds out what the peace of God is like, that passes all our understanding. And that's why Leah left off childbearing until Gad and Asher were born to her maid Zilpah. For truly, unless a man has bridled the pleasure and pain of his senses by abstinence and patience, his affection will never feel inward sweetness and true joy in God and spiritual things. This is Issachar, the fifth son of Leah, who in the story is called *wages*.

And the joy of inward sweetness is well named wages: for this joy is the taste of heavenly bliss, which is the endless wages a devout soul earns, beginning even here. Leah at the birth of this child said, "God has paid me wages because I gave my maid to my husband to bear children." And so it's good that we make our senses bear fruit in abstinence from all kinds of worldly and carnal ease and in patient endurance of all worldly and carnal suffering, for which our Lord in his great mercy gives us unspeakable joy and inward sweetness in our affection, as earnest money toward the sovereign payment of joy we'll get in the high kingdom of heaven.

Jacob said of Issachar that he was a strong ass living between the boundaries.[15] And so it is that a man in this state, who feels in his affection the foretaste of that lasting sweetness and joy, is like an ass, strong, and living between the boundaries. Because no matter how overflowing with spiritual gladness and joy of God he may be, yet, because of the corruption of the flesh in this deathly life he must carry the load of his deathly body, hunger, thirst, cold, and many other hardships. For which he is compared to an ass, in his body; but in his soul he is strong to destroy all discomfort and delight of the flesh by patience and abstinence in his senses and by abundance of spiritual joy and sweetness in the inward feelings. And a soul in this state is

---

15. Gen. 49.14.

living between the boundaries of deathly life and undeathly life. Living between the boundaries he has almost forsaken death, but not fully. Because as long as he still needs this world's goods, as a living man does need food, drink and clothing, he has one foot in this deathly life; and because of the great abundance of spiritual joy and sweetness that he feels in God -- not just now and then, but often -- he has his other foot in undeathly life. That's where I believe St. Paul was when he said this word of great desire, "Who shall free me from this mortal body?"[16] and when he said "I desire to depart, and to be with Christ."[17] And so desires the soul that feels Issachar in his affection, that is to say, that feels the joy of inward sweetness meant by Issachar. Joy urges the soul to forsake this miserable life, but the soul isn't able. It longs to enter the blessed life, but it isn't able. Joy is strong to do what it can do, yet it lives between the boundaries.

### + HOW PERFECT HATRED OF SIN ARISES IN THE AFFECTION +

That's why the next son born after Issachar is Zebulun, that is, hatred of sin. And here is the proper place to say why a man never feels perfect hatred of sin until after he feels the spiritual joy of inward sweetness in his affection. The reason is that until then he doesn't feel the true necessity of such hatred. The actual sensation of holy joy teaches a man what harm sin does to the soul; and after the harm in a soul is felt, much or little, the hatred is in proportion to the harm. Only when a soul by the grace of God and long discipline is come to the experience of holy joy can it feel how sin has been the cause of its delay. And then, when it feels that experience of holy joy slip away because of the flesh's corruption, of which sin is the cause, he awakens to a strong feeling of hatred against all sin and all nature of sin. David teaches us to feel this way when he says in the Psalm, "Be angry, and sin not," or "Rage, and will no sin,"[18] which means: be angry with the sin, but not with nature; because nature moves us to act, but not to sin.

---

16. Rom. 7.14.

17. Phil. 1.23.

18. Ps. 4.5/4.4.

It's important to know that this anger and hatred do not go against charity; on the contrary, charity itself teaches us to feel anger both toward ourselves and toward our fellow Christians. Because a man ought to hate sin in his own nature; and as for our brothers, we ought to hate sin in them, and love them. It's this hatred David is speaking of when he says "I hate them with perfect hatred."[19] And in another Psalm he says "I hate every false way."[20]

Experience confirms that Judah and Issachar were both born before Zebulun was. Because unless a man first actually feel the sensations of love and holy joy there's no way for him to feel this perfect hatred of sin in his will. Judah -- love, or charity -- teaches us that we should hate sin both in ourselves and in others. And Issachar, the spiritual feeling of joy in God, teaches us why we should hate sin. Judah tells us to hate sin and love nature, Issachar to destroy the sin and redeem nature. And that's how it comes about that our nature is made strong in God and in spiritual things, by the perfect hatred and destruction of sin.

For this reason Zebulun is called *a dwellingplace of strength* in the story. And Leah said at his birth, "My husband will dwell in me." And so it is that God, who is the true husband of our soul, dwells in that soul, making it strong in the will by holy joy and sweetness in his love, so that it works eagerly to destroy sin in itself and others by perfect hatred of the sin and all the nature of sin.

That's how Zebulun was born.

## + HOW WELL-ORDERED SHAME RISES
## AND GROWS IN THE AFFECTION +

But granted a soul may feel perfect hatred of sin: may it live without sin? Surely not. And therefore let no man presume. The Apostle says "If we say we have no sin we deceive ourselves, and truth is not in us";[21] St.

---

19. Ps. 138.22/139.21.

20. Ps. 118.128/119.128.

21. I John 1.8.

Augustine too says there is no man living without sin.[22] And I ask you who is there who doesn't sin in ignorance? Yes, and it often happens that God lets the very man fall hard whom he has chosen to correct other men's error, that he learn by his own fall how merciful he ought to be when amending another. And because men often fall grievously into the very sins they hate the most, what springs up in a man's soul after perfect hatred of sin is well-ordered shame.

And so it is that after Zebulun, Dinah is born. Zebulun is hatred of sin and Dinah well-ordered shame of sin. But be sure that if you've never felt Zebulun you've never felt Dinah either. An evil man feels shame, but not this well-ordered shame. Because if he had perfect shame of sin he wouldn't sin so habitually, so wilfully, or so deliberately. But he feels more ashamed of an ugly garment on his body than of an ugly thought in his soul. And if you think you've got Dinah, think whether you'd be as ashamed of an ugly thought in your heart as you'd be if you had to stand naked in front of the king and all the realm. If not, be sure that whatever shame you are capable of feeling isn't well-ordered, if you'd feel it less over your ugly heart than over your ugly body, and if you're more ashamed of your ugly body in the sight of men than you are of your ugly heart in the sight of the king of heaven and all his angels and saints.

There: these are the seven children of Leah, by which are understood seven kinds of affection in a man's soul, which may be either ruled or unruly, measured or unmeasured. When they are ruled and measured they are virtues, and when unruly and unmeasured, vices. A man has to be alert that they be not only ruled but also measured. They are ruled when they come from the thing they should come from, and unruly when they come from the thing they shouldn't come from. And they are measured when they are in the right intensity, but unmeasured if too intense. Because too much fear brings in despair; and too much grief makes a man bitter, and heavy natured, so that he is unable to accept spiritual comfort. And too much hope becomes presumption. And excessive love is flattery and cajolery. And excessive

---

22. Hodgson suggests Augustine's Epistola 157, *Ad Hilarium* (Migne, *Patrologia Latina*, vol. 33, col. 674.)

gladness becomes capricious and dissolute. And untempered hatred of sin is madness. And when they are unruly and unmeasured and thus changed into vices they lose the name of virtues, and can't be counted amongst the sons of Jacob, that is to say, of God. For by Jacob we understand God, as was already shown in the diagram.

## + HOW DISCRETION AND CONTEMPLATION ARISE IN THE REASON +

Thus it becomes clear why we need the virtue of discretion, by which all the others have to be governed: without it they all can turn into vices. This is he, that Joseph, the late-born child. Yet his father loves him more than all the rest because truly without discretion goodness may be neither got nor kept. No wonder if that virtue be singularly loved, without which no other virtue may be had nor governed. But what wonder if this virtue is acquired late? We can't win through to perfect discretion without the habitual practice and hard use of these other affections that come before. For we need first to become habituated in each virtue by itself, and become proficient in them all separately, before we can know them all fully or even be able to make practical judgments about them. And when we eagerly practice these various feelings and visualizations, we often fall and we often get back up. Then by our often falling we can learn how alert we must be to get and keep these virtues. And only thus at some time, by long use, is the soul led to full discretion. And then it may rejoice in the birth of Joseph.

Before this virtue is conceived in a man's soul, everything these other virtues do is done without discretion. And therefore, the more a man presumes and forces himself beyond his strength in any of these spiritual experiences, out of measure, the worse he falls, and fails in his purpose. That's why Dinah is born after all of Leah's sons, and is the last of her children: after a bad fall and a failure we know shame. And thus after many falls and failures, with shame following, a man knows experimentally that there is nothing better than to be ruled by counsel, which is the readiest way to get discretion. Because the man who does everything by counsel will never regret it.[23] Better astute than strong,[24] yes, and prefer the sharper chisel to the bigger mallet.[25] And a prudent man speaks of victories.[26]

Here is the plain reason why neither Leah, nor Zilpah, nor Bilhah could bear such a child, but only Rachel. Because as it is said before, right, or true discretion, comes from reason: Joseph from Rachel. When we first bring forth Joseph in our reason is when we are enabled to do according to counsel what we are stirred to do by inward promptings. This Joseph will know not only what sin we are most stirred to do, but also the weakness of our nature. And according to what either requires, we shall remedy it by seeking direction from those who are wiser than we are and by acting according to them. Otherwise we aren't Joseph, Jacob's son born of Rachel.

More than that: a man not only learns from this Joseph to avoid the deceptions of his enemies, but also, often, may be led by him to perfected knowledge of himself. And precisely according to his knowledge of himself a man may advance in knowing God, of whom he is the image and the likeness. That's why after Joseph, Benjamin is born; for as we understand by Joseph discretion, by Benjamin we understand contemplation. Both are born of the one mother and begotten by the one father. For through the grace of God enlightening our reason we come to full knowledge of our self and of God, that is to say, as full as it can be in this life.

---

23.     *Cf.* Ecclus. 32.24: "My son, do thou nothing without counsel, and thou, halt not repent when thou hast done." Or as Nicolas the clerk tells John the carpenter,
...thus seith Salomon, that was ful trewe,
"Werk al by conseil, and thou shalt nat rewe,"
(*Miller's Tale*, I (A) 3530).
It's Richard's insight that experiment and failure are what prepare us to accept the counsel we won't regret. Experience and authority were usually thought of as opposed alternatives: witness the Wife of Bath.

24.     Richard cites Prov. 16.32, "Melius est vir prudens quam viri forti"; but *cf.* also Wis. 6.1.

25.     This has no source in the Latin. Our Middle English author inserts a saying, "betyr is lyst than lither strength," which Hodgson finds quoted in *The Cloud of Unknowing*, *A Pistle of Preier*, Layamon's *Brut*, *The Owl and the Nightingale*, and elsewhere; it could be translated "better cunning than crude strength" but then it wouldn't be a saying. My introduction of a current saying communicated to me by Professor Jack C. Miller is the greatest license I've taken in this translation.

26.     Richard cites Prov. 21.28, "vir enim prudens loquitur victorias."

But Benjamin is born long after Joseph. Because truly unless we practice long and eagerly in a spiritual struggle that teaches us to know ourselves, we may not be raised up to know and to contemplate God. A man does nothing by lifting his eye to the sight of God if he's not yet able to see himself. First I would desire that a man teach himself to know the unseeable things of his own spirit before he presume to know the unseeable things of the spirit of God. And if a man who doesn't know himself believes that he has attained some partial knowledge of the unseeable things of God, I am sure he is deceived. My advice is that a man first try assiduously to know his own self, which is made in the image and likeness of God.[27]

And be sure that whoever wishes to see God must cleanse his soul, which is like a mirror that when clean shows everything clearly. When a mirror is dirty you can't see anything clearly in it. The same way with your soul: when it's dirty you know neither yourself nor God. When a candle is burning you can see it by its own light, and see other things as well. When your soul burns with the love of God -- that is, when your heart desires the love of God continuously and you can feel it -- is when, by the light of his grace sent through your reason, you can see both your own unworthiness and his great goodness. Clean your mirror, then, and offer your candle to the fire. When it is cleaned and burning, in such a way that you see it with understanding: then a kind of brightness of the light of God begins to shine in your soul and a kind of spiritual sunbeam to appear to your spiritual sight, which is the eye of the soul and is opened so as to behold God and godly things, heaven and heavenly things, and spiritual things of all kinds. This sight is intermittent, here; it comes only when God consents to come down and give it to a working soul in the midst of the struggle of this deathly life. But after this life it will be everlasting. This light was shining in David's soul then he said in the Psalm, "Lord, the light of your face is marked upon us; you have put gladness in my heart."[28] The light of God's face is the shining of his active love, that restores his image in us when it has been disfigured by

---

27. This has no source in the Latin, and the radiant passage that follows takes only hints from its original.

28. Ps. 4.7/4/6.

the darkness of sin. And therefore if a soul burn desiring his light, and feel in itself the certain hope of having what it desires, be sure that it has already conceived Benjamin. What is healthier than the sweetness of this sight, or what more pleasing thing may be felt? Certainly none. And Rachel knew that perfectly well, because reason tells us that compared to this sweetness all other sweetness is sour, and as bitter as gall is after honey.

A man can never come to such grace by his own efforts, because it is the undeserved gift of God; and yet no man can receive it until after he has made mighty efforts in fierce longing. And Rachel knew that perfectly well. And so she multiplies her efforts, and sharpens her longing, and her longing for longing, until at the last, in great abundance of burning desire and the pangs of its delay, Benjamin is born, and his mother Rachel dies. Because when a soul is ravished out of itself by abundance of desire and great multitude of love, so that it is inflamed with the light of the Godhead, all human reason surely dies away.

And therefore whoever you are who desire to come to the contemplation of God, that is to say to bring forth such a child as the story calls Benjamin, meaning the sight of God: use yourself in this manner. Call your thoughts and desires together, and make a church for yourself out of them, and in that congregation teach yourself to love only this good word *Jesus*, so that all your desire and your thought is set only to love Jesus, relentlessly, as much as may be here, so that you fulfill what it says in the Psalm, "Lord, I shall bless thee in the congregations,"[29] that is, in thoughts and desires of the love of Jesus. And then, in this congregation of thoughts and desires, and in this oneness of zeal and of will, look to it that all your thoughts and your desires and your effort and your will be set only to the love and the praise of this Lord Jesus, without any lapse of concentration as long as you are empowered by grace within the limits of your own frailty, humbling yourself ever more to prayer and to counsel, patiently accepting our Lord's will, until the time your mind be ravished out of itself to be fed

---

[29]. Ps. 25.12/26.12; *cf.* also 67.27/68.27, "In the churches bless ye God the Lord."

with the food of angels in the beholding of God and godly things. So it will be fulfilled in you as the Psalm prophesied, "Ibi Beniamyn adolescentulus in mentis excessu," or "There is Benjamin a youth in ecstasy of mind."[30]

+ AMEN +

---

30. Ps. 67.28 in the Vulgate and Douai, which follow the Septuagint; AV 68.27 differs because it follows the Iuxta Hebraos.

  Adam of St. Victor, the poet, conflates the same verse with Jacob's blessing from Genesis 49.27, "Benjamin a ravenous wolf, in the morning shall eat the prey, and in the evening shall divide the spoil":

> Paulus doctor gentium
> Consummavit stadium
> Triumphans in gloria.
>   Hic Benjamin adolescens,
> Lupus, rapax, praeda vescens,
> Hostis est fidelium.
>   Mane lupus, sed ovis vespere.
> Post tenebras lucent sidere:
> Docet evangelium.

"Paul the apostle to the gentiles has run the course and won gloriously. Here Benjamin a youth, a ravenous wolf, devouring the prey, is enemy to the faithful. A wolf at dawn, but a wether by evening. After darkness shine the stars: he teaches the gospel." ("In Conversione Sancti Pauli," in Migne, *Patrologia Latina*, vol. 196, col. 1479.) Adam's meaning is enriched for us if we take one word "adolescens" as a reference, through the Psalm verse and Richard's interpretation of it, to Paul's rapture to the third heaven.

## A NOTE ON THE TRANSLATION

This treatise was among the seven early English mystical treatises printed in 1521 by Henry Pepwell; that book, *The Cell of Self Knowledge*, was edited and published by Edumund F. Gardner in 1910 with modernized spelling and lightly revised vocabulary. A version edited and translated by John Griffiths in *A Letter of Private Direction* (New York: Crossroad, 1981) is streamlined: "As with other texts in this series, the editor and translator has taken short-cuts and condensed where the repetitions and other devices of the originals would only weary or confuse the modern reader." I have not seen the translation that Clifton Wolters is said to have published in England.

For my text I have used the excellent edition by Phyllis Hodgson for the Early English Text Society, *Deonise Hid Divinite and other treatises on contemplative prayer related to The Cloud of Unknowing*: no. 231, London, 1958. For the Latin original of which this treatise is a condensation I have used the edition published by Migne in the *Patrologia Latina* vol. 196 (Paris, 1880), cols. 1-64, and I have consulted its translation by Grover Zinn in the Classics of Western Spirituality series, *Richard of St. Victor: the Twelve Patriarchs* (New York, 1979). For an English Bible I have used the Douai-Rheims version, but since Richard of St. Victor doesn't always follow the Vulgate I have felt free to quote from the Authorized Version, the Revised Standard Version, the Good News Bible, and the Psalter as it appears in the 1979 Book of Common Prayer, or to offer my own paraphrase. I have tried to recreate the qualities my original had when it was new, its freshness, simplicity, sincerity, purposefulness, accessibility, humor, liveliness -- and in so doing I have cultivated a sensation of liberty on my own part. I haven't, for instance, found it at all possible to represent each word of the original by a single word in modern English, but have had to lean with the context on numerous occasions while always aiming for strict fidelity to the meaning as I understand it. Whatever actual licenses I have taken are duly confessed in the notes.

# INTRODUCTION TO THE BRIEFER WORKS

# INTRODUCTION TO THE EPISTLE ON STIRRINGS
# AND
# THE TREATISE ON SPIRITS

In the allegory of the soul's progress as we find it in the *Benjamin Minor* discretion is figured by Joseph, the long-awaited firstborn of Rachel, or reason. The ability to choose between what furthers and what hinders, between the inspiration of the Holy Ghost and the insinuations of our Enemy, Satan, the Accuser -- what you'd think you'd need at the outset of your spiritual journey -- turns out to be the last ability the soul acquires before arriving at contemplation itself. Meanwhile what does one do? Seek good advice is of course an answer, but as the *Benjamin* points out you have to have discretion even to be able to accept what good advice you're offered. Yet we have to act and to decide.

Our author has left two essays that address themselves to the practice of discretion in concrete situations. One is a letter, *An Epistle on Discretion of Stirrings*, written in reply to a young "friend in God" who had asked advice about his eagerness to exercise greater austerities than his fellows; he felt himself stirred to practice "singularities" on his own. The other, *A Treatise on Discretion of Spirits*, is not addressed to any specified audience, but like the *Stirrings* is meant for the use of men or women in holy orders, living by a rule and under the supervision of a confessor.

The impetuous friend himself could see the spiritual danger in his situation -- that's why he wrote for advice in the first place -- and the advice he gets could be summed up intellectually in St. Augustine's "Love God and do what you will." What makes the *Epistle* remarkable is the tact and subtlety with which our author both reproves and heartens -- qualities that arise from the joyous strength of his witness. One feels the steadiness of a man who has been through it all himself; his breathtaking good sense cuts through verbal complexities, so that when he says to love God first and let the eating and fasting take care of themselves it seems what it is, a natural and possible and interesting way to go about it.

In the *Epistle* our author keeps strictly to the questions asked and barely hints that the "singularities" to which the young friend in God aspired would be not only a temptation to spiritual pride in an individual but also a problem of morale and discipline within a religious community. That they would be seems likely enough: men or women cooped up like that, their intensities exacerbated by their all trying to be good, would tend to be vulnerable to rivalries and scandal. Readers of *Piers Plowman* may be surprised to find that the deadly sin of Wrath is embodied, not as a tavern drunk nor a shrewish wife, but as a friar, the convent's gardener who sometimes worked in the kitchen of an aunt who was an abbess. His milieu is the rivalries between friars and priests or between the nuns in a convent; only the monks, by the severity of their rule, make it hard for Wrath to find a lodging place.[1] Our author probably picked up the word "singularities" from St. Bernard, who cautioned against their invidiousness at Clairvaux. And in the Treatise on Discretion of Spirits, addressed not to a single friend but to a more general audience who could share the brunt, our author allows himself a more heated attack against these observances inspired, as he says, by the Fiend disguised as an angel.

The *Treatise* takes its start from passages in a pair of sermons Bernard had preached on successive days: *Of the Seven Spirits* and *Of the Multiple Efficacy of the Divine Word*.[2] Our author takes from Bernard the idea that we need to distinguish between the evil and good spirits, resisting the former who reveal who they are by what they insinuate; but then where Bernard merely goes on to exhortations that we give our full attention to the good, our author goes into the subtle psychology of discernment, conscience, and confession. I don't think it matters much whether or not we believe in Satan, or that the world and the flesh have spirits that can tempt or possess us; we can follow the argument well enough if we regard them as fictions like the id,

---

1.   B. v. 135 ff.

2.   Sermones De Diversis 23 & 24 in *Sancti Bernardi Opera* (Rome, 1970) vol. 6, 1, pp. 178-86. (*PL* vol. 183, cols. 600-605.)

the animus, or the Spectre of Urthona. After all we do have stirrings that sometimes occur to us verbally, like immaterial voices. Some of them do urge us to pleasure, ambition or malice. And we have a choice between agreeing with them or resisting them unless, as our authors warn us, we become their slaves and take on their office ourselves.

Since I don't know anything about the intimate psychology of confession, I can't comment on our author's idea that a thorough shriving cleans our soul's slate, so that for a time all our inner urges come from God or the Devil, the assent only being ours. I have enough faith in our author's sincerity to believe he's describing something he knows about from experience, but my own experience doesn't suffice for me to understand the description.

I do want to say something about the style of the *Treatise*, which is hortatory and repetitious, and even somewhat clumsy at times, though a good orator reading it aloud to a group could get it over. In a few places I've changed word order, slightly condensed, or divided long sentences, in the interests of intelligibility; and sometimes I've had to use several different words for one that is repeated relentlessly through changing contexts, because there's no Modern English word that has the same semantic range as the one in the text; but mainly I've left such things as I found them even if they did seem clumsy or repetitious. I believe that the many repetitions serve not a rhetorical purpose but a moral one. They require of us a kind of patience, an acknowledgement that our having heard something once doesn't mean we now understand it and can afford to skip over: they require the humility, in one word, that we must absolutely have if we're to understand a single word of what's written here.

# AN EPISTLE ON DISCRETION OF STIRRINGS

# AN EPISTLE ON DISCRETION OF STIRRINGS

Spiritual friend in God: that same grace and joy I desire for myself, I desire for you at God's will. You ask my advice about silence and speaking, about eating with others and fasting on your own, about living in company and about keeping solitude by yourself. And you say you are confused about what to do, since you say on the one hand you are held back by speaking, by eating with others as they do, and by living in company; but on the other hand you are afraid to be strictly still, singular in fasting and alone in living, as presumption of being more holy than you are, and for many other dangers. Because often nowadays those who most keep silence, fast singly, and live alone are thought the holiest and are in the greatest danger.

And they are indeed the holiest if grace alone is the cause of their silence, their fasting and their solitude while nature merely consents passively. But otherwise there's nothing but danger on all sides. Because it's dangerous to constrain one's nature to any such work of devotion as silence or speech, eating with others or singular fasting, living in company or alone (I mean beyond ordinary custom and the course of nature and training), unless nature be led there by grace: and namely to such works as are in themselves indifferent, that is to say, now good and now bad, now for you and now against you, now a help and now a hindrance. Because it might happen, if you followed your singular stirring and constrained yourself to strict silence, to individual fasting, or to a solitary life, that you would often be still when you ought to speak up, often fast when you ought to eat, often be alone when you ought to be in company: or if you allowed yourself to speak up whenever you felt like it, to dine in commons, and to live in company, then perhaps you would sometimes speak when you ought to keep still, eat when you ought to go hungry, and be in company when you ought to be alone. Thus you could easily fall into error, to the great confusion not only of your own soul but also of others. And therefore, wishing to avoid such error, in your letter you ask me two things: the first is my conception of you and your stirrings, and the other is my counsel in this case, and in all such cases when they occur.

As for the first, my answer is that I hesitate in this matter and in others like it to put forth my crude conception, such as it is, for two reasons. And one is this: I can't be entirely sure of it, to claim that it's unshakably true. The other is: your own inward disposition that you speak of in your letter, and the aptitude you have for all these things, aren't yet so fully known to me as they'd have to be if I were to give full advice in this case. Because as the Apostle says, "Nemo nouit que sunt hominis nisi spiritus hominis, qui in ipso est"; "Nobody knows the secret dispositions of man except the spirit of that same man himself."[1]

And maybe you yourself don't know your own inward disposition as fully yet as you will in time, when God will teach it to you by experience, among many fallings and risings. For I never yet knew a sinner to achieve full knowledge of himself and his inward disposition, unless he learned it first in God's school by being often tested and by many fallings and risings. Our soul is like a poor ship between the waves and the floods and the storms of the sea on the one hand, and a gentle wind, calms and temperate weather on the other, that makes landfall at last and finds its haven: between the temptations and tribulations that afflict a soul in this ebbing and flowing life (like the storms and floods on the one hand) and the grace and the goodness of the Holy Ghost, the manifold visitation, sweetness and empowering of spirit (like the gentle wind and temperate weather on the other) the poor soul, like the ship, arrives at last at the landfall of stability and the haven of well-being, which is the clear and steady knowledge of himself and of all his inward dispositions; through which knowledge he is seated quietly in himself, like a king crowned in his realm, governing himself powerfully, wisely, and well in all his thoughts and stirrings, both in body and in soul.

The wise man describes a man like that when he says: "Beatus vir qui suffert temptationem, quoniam cum probatus fuerit accipiet coronam vitae,

---

[1]. 1 Corinthians 2.11.

quam repromisit Deus diligentibus se"; "He is a blessed man who endures trials patiently, because when he has been tested he shall take the crown of life which God has promised to all who love him."[2] The crown of life may be interpreted two ways. One way is as spiritual wisdom, full discretion, and perfection of virtue which may be attained by grace in this life; these three knit together may be called a crown of life. The other way the crown of life may be interpreted is as the endless joy that each true soul shall have after this life in the bliss of heaven. And surely a man may not achieve either of these crowns unless he first be tested by enduring distress and temptation, as this same text says: "Quoniam cum probatus fuerit, accipiet coronam vitae"; that is, "When he has been tested he shall take the crown of life." As if saying according to my understanding touched on before: a sinful man must first be tested in diverse trials, now rising, now falling, falling by weakness, rising by grace; otherwise he shall never in this life receive from God spiritual wisdom in clear knowledge of himself and of his inward dispositions, nor full discretion in teaching and counseling others, nor yet the third blessing, which is perfection of virtue in loving God and his brother.

All these three -- wisdom, discretion, and perfection of virtue -- are one thing, and they may be called the crown of life. A crown is made of three things. Gold is the first, precious stones the second, and turrets of fleur-de-lys, raised up above the head, are the third. I understand by gold wisdom, by precious stones discretion, and by turrets of fleur-de-lys the perfection of virtue. God encompasses the head; and by wisdom we govern our spiritual works on every side. Precious stones give light so men can see; and by discretion we teach and counsel our brothers. The turrets of fleur-de-lys have two side branches, one reaching to the right and one to the left, and a third rising straight up above the head; and by perfection of virtue, which is charity, we mean two side branches of love, which reach out, towards our friends on the right and our enemies on the left, while one (above man's understanding, which is the head of the soul) goes straight up towards God. This is the crown of life, which may be got by grace here in this life.

---

2.     James 1.12.

So be lowly in your struggle, and submit meekly to be tested until you are proved. Because once you have been proved you shall receive either this crown here or the other there, or both. And there are many who have been upheld by grace in their trials here and yet never come to the crown that may be had in this life; who, if they continue meekly and await patiently the will of Our Lord, shall receive the other abundantly in the bliss of heaven. This crown that may be got here seems glorious to you. Yea, carry yourself as humbly as you can with the help of grace, because it compared to the other is like one noble compared to a world full of gold. I say all this to give you comfort and evidence of strength in the spiritual struggle you have undertaken trusting in Our Lord.

And I tell you all this so you can see how far you still are from truly knowing your own inward disposition, and to warn you not to give place too soon nor follow the singular stirrings of your young heart when you may be self-deceived. I tell you all this to give you my conception of you and of your stirrings, as you asked me. Because I can see that you are very apt and greedily disposed toward such sudden urges to do things on your own, and stubborn to cling to them when they come to you; and that is full of danger.

I don't say that this aptitude and greedy disposition in you, nor in any other disposed as you are, no matter how dangerous, is evil in itself; no, I don't say that. God forbid that you take it that way! On the contrary, I say that it is wholly good in itself, and a great aptitude for perfection, yes, and for the greatest perfection there can be in this life; it can be, if a soul disposed that way will assiduously, night and day, humble itself to God and to good counsel, and strongly rise up to martyr itself, casting down its own ideas and its own desires in all such sudden and singular stirrings, and say sharply that it will not follow such stirrings, seem they never so pleasing, so deep, nor so holy, unless they have the confirmation and consent of spiritual teachers (I mean such as have long experience of the solitary life). Through spiritual perseverance in this meekness such a soul may deserve, by grace and by the experience gained in this spiritual battle with itself, to win the crown of life mentioned earlier.

This inward disposition, such a great potential for good in a soul that is humbled as I say, is an equally great danger in another soul that will follow the stirrings of its greedy heart impetuously, according to its own idea and desire without advice of counsel. And so for the love of God be careful with this capacity and with this inward disposition I speak of, if it be in you as I describe it, and make yourself continually meek to prayer and to counsel. Break down your own idea and your desire in all such sudden and individual stirrings, and don't follow them lightly until you know where they come from and whether they are fitting for you or not.

As to my perception of your stirrings, and the advice you ask: I have to say that I perceive them with suspicion that they might be conceived apewise. They say an ape does what he sees another do. Forgive me if my suspicion is mistaken, I beg you. I am impelled to tell you this by the love I have for your soul because recently one of our spiritual brothers in your country was touched by those same urges to strict silence, singular fasting, and complete solitude -- apewise, as he conceded when after long communing with me he had put himself and his stirrings to the test. It happened, as he said, because he had seen a man in your country who is always, as is well known, in great silence, singular fasting, and solitude. And I am surely convinced that his are true stirrings, caused only by grace that moves him inwardly and not by any outward sight or report of any other man's silence -- which would be called apely, as I say in my simple thought.

So be wary, and test your urges and where they come from. For how you are stirred, whether from within by grace or from without apewise, God knows, not I. Nevertheless, I can say this to you, in shunning danger like this: make sure you're not being an ape; that is to say, make sure your urges to silence or to speaking, to fasting or to eating, to loneliness or company, come from within, from abundance of love and devotion in spirit, and not from without by windows of your bodily senses, your ears and your eyes; for, as Jeremiah says clearly, "By such windows death comes in," "Mors intrat per fenestras,"[3] And this suffices, little as it is, for answer to your first question, my conception of you and of your stirrings, that you asked me in your letter.

---

3. Jeremiah 9.21: "For death is come up through our windows, it is entered into our houses to destroy the children from without, the young men from the streets."

As to the second question, where you ask me my advice in this case and others like it when they happen: I beseech Almighty Jesus, as he is called the "Angel of Great Counsel,"[4] that he of his mercy be your advisor and encourager in all your distress and need, and guide me by his wisdom to fulfill in part by my teaching, simple as it is, the trust of your heart, which you offer me ahead of many another, a simple ignorant wretch as I am unworthy to teach you or any other for littleness of grace and for lack of learning. Nevertheless, in spite of my ignorance, I shall say something, answering to your desire according to my simple ability, with trust in God that his grace be teacher and guide, when mother wit and learning both fall short.

You know well yourself that neither silence in itself nor speaking, singular fasting nor eating with others, solitude nor company, all these things nor any of them, is the true end of our desire. To some men, but not to all, they are means towards that end, if they be done according to rule and discretion; and otherwise they are more hindrance than help. And therefore I don't recommend at this time that you make a full commitment to speech nor silence, eating nor fasting, company nor solitude: because perfection is not in them. But I can give you some advice in general to govern yourself by in these stirrings and in all others like them, whenever you find two contraries such as silence and speaking, fasting and eating, solitude and company, ordinary clothing of Christian men's religion and the special habits of diverse and distinct brotherhoods, and so on -- which are in themselves only works of nature and mankind.

You have it both innately and by your rule for your outer man now to speak and now be still, now eat and now fast, be now in company and now alone, wear now ordinary clothing and now a particular habit, whenever you wish to and when you see that any of them will help nourish the heavenly grace working in your soul, unless -- God forbid! -- you or another be so ignorant and so blinded in the sorrow-bringing temptations of the noonday devil[5] that you bind yourself by some perverted vow to your own special form

---

4.  Isaiah 9.6 in the Septuagint and the Vetus Itala [Hodgson].

5.  Midday devil: the *daemonium meridianum* of Psalm 90.6: [thou shalt not be afraid] "of the arrow that flieth in the day, of the business that walketh about in the dark: of

of living, under color of pretended holiness in holy-seeming bondage, to the full and final destruction of the freedom of Christ, which is the spiritual garment of the supreme holiness that is possible in this life or in the other, by the witness of Paul who says "Vbi spiritus Domini, ibi libertas": "Where the spirit of God is, is where freedom is."[6]

Now when you see that all such works contrary to each other may be both good and evil in their use, I beg you leave them both, because that is the easiest thing for you to do if you wish to be humble. And leave off the busy scanning and prying in your wits to see which is better. But do this: set the one on one hand and the other on the other, and choose a thing that is hidden between them; when you have that it gives you leave, in freedom of spirit, to begin and cease doing either of them at your own pleasure, without any blame.

But now you ask me what is that thing. I shall tell you what I have in mind that it is. It is God for whom you should be still, if you should be still; and for whom you should speak, if you should speak; and for whom you should fast, if you should fast; and for whom you should eat, if you should eat; and for whom you should be alone; if you should be alone, and for whom you should be in company, if you should be in company; and so forth for all the rest, whatever they are. For silence isn't God, and speaking isn't God; fasting isn't God, and eating isn't God; solitude isn't God, and company isn't God; nor yet any of all other such pairs of contraries. He is hidden between them, and may not be found by any effort of your soul, but only by the love of your heart. He may not be known by reason. He may not be thought, got, nor tracked down by understanding. But he may be chosen and loved by the true, loving will of your heart. Choose him; and then you are silently speaking and speakingly silent, fastingly eating and eatingly fasting, and so forth through all the rest.

Choosing God by love that way, wisely cutting loose so as to seek him out with the clean will of a true heart between all such pairs of contraries,

---

invasion or of the noonday devil." AV Psalm 91.6 has "the destruction that wasteth at midday."

6.     2 Corinthians 3.17.

rejecting them both when they come and offer themselves to be the point and aim of our spiritual contemplation, is the best way of tracking and searching after God that may be achieved or learned in this life (I mean, the life of a soul who intends to be a contemplative); yea, even though a soul that hunts this way never sees anything that may be perceived by the spiritual eye of reason. For if God be what you love and what you have in your mind, the main thing and the point of your heart, that is enough for you in this life though you never see more of him with the eye of reason your whole lifetime. Such a blind shot with the sharp dart of longing can never miss the mark, which is God; as he says himself in the *Book of Love*, where he speaks to a languishing and loving soul this way: "Vulnerasti cor meum, soror mea, amica mea, sponsa mea, vulnerasti cor meum in vno oculorum tuorum"; "You have wounded my heart, my sister, my darling, my bride, you have wounded my heart in one of your eyes."[7] The soul has two eyes, reason and love. By reason we may see his tracks and know how mighty, how wise, and how good he is -- in his creatures, but not in himself. But whenever reason falls short, love comes into play; because by love we can find him, feel him, and hit him even in himself. It is a wonderful eye, love, for Our Lord says of a loving soul: "You have wounded my heart in one of your eyes"; that is to say, in love that is blind to many things and sees only that one thing it seeks; and therefore it tracks and sights, hits and wounds the point it aims for sooner than it would if sight were divided by looking at many things, as it is when the reason searches and ransacks among all such separate things as these: silence and speaking, eating with others or singular fasting, solitude or company, and all such, to decide which is better.

Leave off this way of doing, I beg you, and pretend you don't even know that there are any such means to get God by; because really there aren't, if you wish to be a true contemplative and soon achieve your aim. And therefore I beg you and others like you, saying with the Apostle "Videte vocationem vestram, et in ea vocatione qua vocatus estis, state"; "See your calling, and in that calling where you are called, stand," firm, and wait in the

---

7. Song of Solomon 4.9.

name of Jesus.[8] Your calling is to be a true contemplative, and your example is Mary, Martha's sister. Do then as Mary did. Set the point of your heart on one thing. "Porro vnum est necessarium"; "But one thing is necessary," which is God.[9] Him you would have; him you seek, him you wish to love; him you wish to experience; him you wish to hold yourself to; and you won't do that by silence nor by speaking, by singular fasting nor by eating with others, by solitude nor by living in company. Because sometimes silence is good, but at that same time speaking would be better; and on the other hand sometimes speaking is good, but at that same time silence would be better; and so forth of all the rest, fasting, eating, solitude, company, and all the like. For sometimes the one is good, but the other is better; but neither of them is any time the best. And therefore let be good all that is good, and better all that is better, for both will fail and have an end; and choose, with Mary your example, the best, that never will fall short. "Maria, inquit optimus, optimam partem elegit, que non auferetur ab ea." The best is Almighty Jesus, and he said that Mary, the mirror of all contemplatives, had chosen the best, which should never be taken from her. And therefore, I beg you, with Mary leave the good and the better, and choose the best.

Let them be, all such things -- silence and speaking, fasting and eating, solitude and company, and all such -- and pay no attention to them. You don't know what they mean, and, I beg you, don't covet that knowledge. And if you think or speak of them at any time then think and say that they are so high and such worthy things of perfection -- to have the art of speaking or of being still, to have the art of fasting and of eating, to have the art of solitude and of company -- that it would be a mere folly and a foul presumption in such a weak wretch as you are to meddle with such great perfection. Because to speak and to be still, to eat and to fast, to be alone and to be in company whenever we decide to, we may have by nature; but we can't have the art of them except by grace.

---

8. I Corinthians 7.20.

9. Luke 10.42.

And without doubt such grace is never achieved by any such means as the strict silence, singular fasting, or solitary dwelling that you speak of, which are caused from without by occasion of hearing about or seeing another man in such singular doings. But if this grace shall ever be got, it has to be learned from within, from God whom you have eagerly longed for with all the love of your heart for many a day, utterly emptying your spiritual vision of all sight of any thing beneath him, even though some of those things that I bid you thus empty out may seem in some men's sight entirely worthy means to get God by. Yea, let men say what they will, but you do as I tell you, and let the proof be witness. Because to him who will succeed spiritually one means is enough, and he needs nothing but the active thought of good God only, with a reverent stirring of lasting love: so long as that means to God get you nothing but God, and so long as you keep your stirring of love whole, that you can feel by grace in your heart, and don't scatter your spiritual attention.

Then the very thing you feel will tell you when to speak and when to be still. And it will govern you discriminatingly in all your living without any error, and teach you secretly how you shall begin and end in all such natural doings with a great and sovereign discretion. Because if you are able by grace to keep it habitually and in continual use, then whenever it's needful for you to speak, or to eat with others, or to live in company, or to do any other thing that belongs to the ordinary true custom of Christian men and of nature, it will first stir you softly to speak, or to do whatever other ordinary thing of nature; and then, if you don't do it, it will hit you like a stab in heart and trouble you and give you no peace unless you do it. And in same way, if you are speaking or doing any other such work common to the course of nature, whenever it be needful and helpful to you to be still and to apply yourself to the contrary, as fasting is to eating, solitude to company, and all such other, which are works of singular holiness, it will stir you to them.

So by experience of such a blind stirring of love towards God a contemplative soul comes sooner to the grace of discretion, to have the art of speaking and of being still, to have the art of eating and of fasting, to have the art of company and of solitude, and all the like, than it could by any such singularities as you speak of, undertaken according to the stirrings of a man's own understanding and his will from within himself or yet by the example of another man's doing from without, whatever it is. Because such strained doings after the stirrings of nature, without the stirrings of grace, are just pain without profit -- except to those in holy orders who are enjoined to undertake them in penance, where profit rises only because of obedience and not by the strictness of doing; beyond that, it's nothing but trouble for all who try it. But to will lovingly and eagerly to have God is great and exceeding ease, true spiritual peace, and an early taste of eternal tranquility.

And therefore speak when you please and stop when you please; eat when you pleas and fast when you please; be in company when you please and be by yourself when you please: so long as God and grace be your guide. Let fast who will, and be alone who will, and be silent who will; but you keep with God, who beguiles no man. Because silence and speaking, fasting and eating, solitude and company, may all beguile. And if you hear of any man who speaks or of any who is still, of any who eats or of any who fasts, or of any who is in company or else is by himself, think and say, if you will, that they know how to do as they ought to do, unless the contrary shows openly. But don't you do as they do; I mean, because they do, apewise. Because you don't know how, nor are you disposed as they are. And so quit working according to other men's dispositions; and work according to your own, if you are able to know what it is. And until the time when you are able to know what it is, work according to the advice of men who know their own disposition, but not according to their disposition. Because such men and no one else should give advice in such cases. And this suffices for an answer to all your letter. The grace of God be evermore with you, in the name of Jesus. Amen.

# A TREATISE ON DISCRETION OF SPIRITS

## A TREATISE ON DISCRETION OF SPIRITS

There are several kinds of spirits, and we need to know how to discriminate between them, since we are taught by the Apostle St. John not to believe them all.[1] It may seem to some, lacking wisdom and inexpert in holy things, that every thought a man hears in his heart would be the speech of his own spirit, not any other. But both faith and the witness of Holy Scripture clearly prove otherwise. "I will hear," says the prophet David, (not what I speak myself, but) "what my Lord God speaks in me."[2] And another prophet says that an angel spoke in him.[3] And we are taught in the psalm that wicked spirits send evil thoughts into men.[4] And in addition to these there is a spirit of the flesh that is not good, as the Apostle Paul shows clearly where he says that some men are blown up with the spirit of their flesh.[5] He also declares plainly that this world has a spirit, where he rejoices in God, not only for himself but also for his disciples, because they had not taken that spirit of the world but the spirit sent from God, which is the Holy Ghost.[6]

---

1. I John 4.1-6: "Dearly beloved, believe not every spirit, but try the spirits if they be of God: because many false prophets are gone out into the world."

2. Psalm 84.9/85.8.

3. Zechariah 1.9.

4. Psalm 77.45/78.45: "And he sent upon them the wrath of his indignation: indignation and wrath and trouble, which he sent by his evil angels."

5. Colossians 2.18: "Let no man seduce you, willing in humility, and religion of angels, walking in the things which he hath not seen, in vain puffed up by the sense of his flesh."

6. I Corinthians 2.12: "Now we have received not the spirit of this world, but the Spirit which is of God; that we may know the things that are given to us from God."

And these two spirits of the flesh and the world are, as it were, servants or sergeants of that cursed spirit, the foul fiend of hell; the spirit of wickedness is the lord of the spirits of the flesh and of the world. And if any of these three spirits speak to our spirit, we should not believe them, because they never speak except to lead us to lose both our body and our soul.

The spirit that speaks to our spirit declares which one it is by what it says. The spirit of the flesh speaks always about pleasant things, easeful to the body; the spirit of the world about vain things and greed for honor; and the spirit of the fiend about cruel and bitter things. Whenever a thought that strikes our heart has to do with food, drink, and sleep, with soft clothing, lechery, or any other such things that pertain to the business of the flesh, and inflames our heart with desire for such things, we can be sure that it is the spirit of the flesh speaking. And therefore we put him away the best we can by grace, for he is our adversary. Whenever any thought that strikes our heart has to do with the vain joy of this world, and kindles in us a desire to be thought fair and favored, to be thought great in name and in knowledge, to be thought wise and worthy, or else to have great rank and responsibility in this life (such thoughts and all others, which would make a man seem deep and distinguished, not only in the sight of others but also in his own self-esteem), there can be no doubt it's the spirit of the world that speaks all this, a far more dangerous enemy than the spirit of the flesh and one that should be the more strenuously fended off. And it sometimes happens that these two servants and sergeants of the foul fiend (who is the spirit and prince of wrath and of wickedness) are either stoutly put down and trodden under foot by grace and a soul's spiritual agility; but often they are deceitfully withdrawn by the cunning of their malicious master, the foul fiend of hell, because he plans to rise himself with great malice and wrath, like a lion running wild to savage the frailty of our poor simple souls.[7] And this happens whenever the thought of our heart stirs us, not to the pleasures of our flesh, nor yet to the vain joy of this world, but to grumbling, grouching, and complaining, to bitterness of soul, distress and impatience, anger and melancholy, to ill will, hatred, envy, and all that kind of misery. It makes us act and feel heavy if

---

7.   *Cf.* I Peter 5.8.

anything be done or said to us less pleasantly and wisely than we think it ought to be. It arouses all evil suspicion; it makes us grab at any sign or expression we notice, any word or work that can any way be turned to malice or heaviness of heart.

We should resist these thoughts, that would put us out of peace and tranquility of heart, as if they were the fiend of hell himself, and flee from them as we would from perdition. No doubt the other thoughts, insinuated by the spirits of the flesh and the world, work any way they can for the loss of our soul: but this spirit of malice is the most dangerous. He by himself, but not the other two without him. Because no matter how clean a soul is from the lusts of the flesh and vain joy of this world, if it is yet befouled with this spirit of malice, of wrath, and of wickedness, all other prior cleanliness notwithstanding, it is losable. And no matter how befouled a soul is with the lusts of the flesh and vain joy of this world, if by grace it keep itself in restfulness of heart and in peace with its fellow Christians (however hard that may be to do while the habits of the other two persist), it is less losable, foulness of the flesh and the world notwithstanding. And therefore, though all the pleasant thoughts of our foul flesh are evil, since they rob the soul of its pleasure in devotion; and though the vain joy of this world is worse, since it robs us of the true joy we should have in contemplation of heavenly things, ministered and taught to us by the angels of heaven (because whoever desires to be honored, favored and served by men here on earth deserves to forego the honor, favor and service of angels in spiritual contemplation of heaven and heavenly things all their lifetime, which is better and more worthy in itself than even the joy and enjoyment of devotion); yet I call the spirit of malice, of wrath, and of wickedness the worst spirit of them all. And why? Because it robs us of the best thing of all: that is charity, which is God.

Because whoever doesn't have peace and restfulness in his heart won't have the lively presence of the lovely sight of heaven's high peace either, good gracious God, his own dear self. David witnesses this in the Psalm, where he says that God's place is peace and his abode in Zion.[8] Zion is as much as to say the sight of peace. The sight of the soul is the thought of the

---

8. Psalm 75.3/76.2.

same soul. And surely God has made his abode in the soul that most is occupied in peaceful thoughts. He says so himself by the prophet when he says: "Upon whom shall my spirit rest, if not the meek and the tranquil?"[9]

And therefore whoever would have God dwelling in him continually, and live in charity and within sight of the deep tranquility of the Godhead, which is the deepest and best part of contemplation that may be had in this life, must be wary night and day to put down the spirits of the flesh and the world, when they come, but wariest against the spirit of malice, wrath and wickedness, because he is the foulest and the worst defilement of all.

We need to know his wiliness not to be caught out by his calamitous deceit. Because sometimes that devil, wicked and cursed as he is, will change his likeness into that of an angel of light, so that under color of virtue he may do the more harm.[10] But even then, if we look diligently, we can see that all he shows us is the seed of bitterness and discord, no matter how holy and fair it seem at the first showing. He stirs many into singular acts of holiness, beyond their common rule and custom and capacity, such as fasting, hair shirts, and many other devout observances and outward doings, to be an open reproach of other men's shortcomings, which is none of their business. He urges them to do all this under color of devotion and of charity; not that he is so delighted by any act of devotion or charity, but that he loves dissension and slander, which is the usual result of such unseemly singularities. Because whenever one or two members of a devout congregation practice any such outward singularities, then in the sight of all fools the rest are disgraced by them; but in the sight of wise men they are the ones who are disgraced. But the fools outnumber the wise men, so the favor of fools makes these singular doers think they are wise, when, if it were judged wisely, they and all their group would be seen as plain fools and darts shot by the devil to kill true simple souls under color of love and salvation. And in this way the fiend

---

9. Dom Noetinger, the *Le Nuage de l'Inconnaisance* (Tours, 1925), p. 317n, identifies the quotation as Isaiah 46.2. The Vulgate reading is *ad quem respiciam, nisi ad pauperculum et contritum spiritu*; our author has translated from the *"Version antique"* as he found it in the Fathers and St. Bernard, *super quem respiciam, nisi humilem et quietum*.

10. II Corinthians 11.14: "And no wonder, for Satan himself transformeth himself into an angel of light."

brings in many deceits. Whoever won't agree to them, but humbles himself truly to prayer and to counsel, will be saved from all these wiles by grace.

But it's sad to say, and worse to feel, that sometimes our own spirit is so overcome, perhaps, with each of these three spirits of the flesh, the world, and the devil, and so brought under their power, in bondage and addiction as slave to them all, that it is a grief to know it -- in great confusion and loss of itself, it takes on itself, against itself, the office of each one of these spirits. And this happens when, after long use and habitually giving in to them when they come, our own spirit is made so fleshly, so worldly, and so malicious, so wicked, and so contrary, that now entirely of itself, without the suggestion of any other spirit, it engenders and brings forth in itself not only lustful thoughts of the flesh and vain thoughts of the world, but, worst of all, bitter and wicked thoughts, backbiting and judging and evil suspicion toward others.

And when our spirit is in such a state, I believe it's hard to know whether it is our own spirit that is speaking, or whether it is hearing one of the other three spirits speak within itself, as we have said before. But why do we need to care who speaks, when it is all one and one thing that is spoken? If it be your enemy, don't give in to him, but humble yourself to prayer and counsel; and that way you can stoutly stand against him. If it be your own spirit, scold him harshly, and grieve miserably that you ever fell into such great misery as to be a miserable slave of the devil. Make confession of your habitual giving in and of your old sin; in that way you may be enabled by grace to regain your freedom.

And in this grace-given freedom you can soon come to know wisely and tell verifiably whether it is your own spirit that speaks these evils, or other, evil, spirits that speak them in you. Knowing that may become a powerful means and help in withstanding them, because often ignorance causes wavering, and knowledge causes faith; and I'll tell you how you can gain this knowledge. When in doubt or perplexity as to whether these evil thoughts are the speech of your own spirit or one of the others who are your enemies, diligently inquire of your confessor and your own conscience to see whether you have been shrived, according to the judgment of your confessor, of all occasions when you ever gave in to the kind of sin that is perplexing you. And if you haven't been shrived, shrive yourself as truly as you can by grace and by counsel. And then you can be sure that all the thoughts that come to you after you have been shrived, stirring you to the same sins again, are not the words of your own spirit, but of those other three. And you are not to blame for any such thoughts, however thick, foul, and many they may be, when they first come in, unless you are careless in withstanding them. And if you withstand them stiffly you may earn not only release from the purgatory that you had already deserved for the same sins done before, but also much grace in this life and much reward in the bliss of heaven.

When all these evil thoughts are coming in to you, stirring you to any sin, and you have consented to them -- before you feel sorrow for that consent, but when you are ready to be confessed: there is no danger in taking them to yourself and confessing them as thoughts of your own spirit. But to take to yourself other thoughts, when you know by the sure proof shown you before that they are speeches of other spirits than yourself: in that there is great danger. Because in that way you might easily tyrannize your conscience, weighing it down with something as a sin when it isn't a sin. And this would be a great mistake and lead to the greatest danger. Because if it were true that every evil thought and stirring to sin were the work and the speech of no other spirit but a man's own, then it would follow that a man's own spirit were a fiend, which is plainly false and damnable madness. Even though a soul may, by weakness and habit of sinning, fall into so much wretchedness that it binds itself to do the office of the devil, stirring itself to sin ever more and more without any suggestion from any other spirit, it still isn't a devil in its nature. It is a devil in works and may be called devilish, for it is like the devil in what it does, namely urging itself to sin which is the office of the devil. Just the same, in spite of all its bondage in sin and devilish office, it may by grace of contrition, confession and amending get its freedom back and be made savable, yea, and a special saint of God's in this life, when it was damnable before and cursed in the living.

And therefore, dangerous as it is for a soul that is fallen into sin not to burden his conscience with it nor amend himself of it, it is just as dangerous, and if it may be said, even more dangerous, for a man to burden his conscience with every thought and stirring to sin that will come into him.

Because by such foolish overburdening of conscience he may easily run into wandering of conscience, and by that be led to despair his whole lifetime. And this is all caused by not knowing discretion of spirits, which anyone may learn by practice if he will look closely right after his soul has been truly cleansed by confession, as has been described already.

Because just after confession a soul is like a clean sheet of paper in its capacity to receive what men will write on it. Both sides press in to write on it when it is made clean in itself by confession, God and his angels on one side and the fiend and his angels on the other. But the soul has the free choice to receive whichever it will. The soul's receiving is its consent. A new thought and a stirring to any sin, which you have rejected before in your confession: what else is that but one of the three spirits, your enemies, proffering to write on your soul the same sin again. It isn't the speech of your own self, because there is no such thing written in your soul: all that was washed away in your confession, and your soul was left naked and bare, with nothing but a frail and a free consent, inclining more to the foreaccustomed evil than it is to the good, but more apt to the good than to the evil because of its cleanness and the power of the sacrament of confession. But of itself it has nothing whereby it can think or stir itself to good or to evil; and therefore it follows that whatever thought comes into it, whether it be good or evil, is not of itself. But the consent to the good or the evil, whichever it is, is always the work of the same soul.

And according to the excellence or the wretchedness of this consent it deserves thereafter its pain or bliss. If its consent be to evil, then immediately it has by encumbrance of sin taken on the office of that same spirit that first made him the suggestion of that same sin. And if it be to the good, then immediately it has by grace taken on the office of that same spirit that first made him the stirring to that same good. Whenever our mind receives any thought tending to our salvation, say of chastity, of soberness, of despising the world, of voluntary poverty, of patience, of humility, or of charity, without doubt it is the spirit of God that speaks, either by himself or else by some of his angels: that is to say, either his angels of this life, who are the true teachers, or else his angels in bliss, who are true stirrers and inspirers of good.

And as we have seen that a soul may, by long use and habitual consenting to the three other, evil, spirits, be made so fleshly, so worldly, and so malicious that it takes upon itself their office, we can also see that a soul may, by long use and habit in goodness, be made so spiritual by cleanness of living and devotion of spirit against the spirit of the flesh, and so heavenly against the spirit of the world, and so godly by peace and by charity and by restfulness of heart against the spirit of malice, wrath and wickedness, that all such good thoughts now belong to it by office, to think when it please him without distraction, in as great perfection as the frailty of this life will allow.

And so it may be seen how each thought that strikes our hearts, whether good or evil, is not always the speech of our own spirit; but the consent to the thought, whatsoever it may be, is always our own. Jesus grant us by his grace to consent to the good and to withstand the evil. Amen.

## STUDIES IN MEDIAEVAL LITERATURE

1. J. Elizabeth Jeffrey, **Blickling Spirituality and the Old English Vernacular Homily**
2. Ronald Pepin, **Literature of Satire in the Twelfth Century:** *A Neglected Mediaeval Genre*
3. Aileen Ann Macdonald, **The Figure of Merlin in Thirteenth-Century French Romance**
4. Jillian M. Hill, **Medieval Debate on Jean De Meung's** *Roman de la Rose*
5. Ronald G. Koss, **Family, Lineage and Kinship in the** *Cycle de Guillaume d'Orange*
6. George Bond, **The *Pearl* Poem: An Introduction and Interpretation**
7. Richard of St. Victor, **Richard Of St. Victor's** *Treatise Of The Study Of Wisdom That Men Call Benjamin*: **As Adapted In Middle English By The Author of** *The Cloud Of Unknowing* **Together with** *Treatise on Discretion of Spirits* **and** *Epistle on Discretion of Stirrings*, Dick Barnes (trans.)

www.ingramcontent.com/pod-product-compliance
Lightning Source LLC
Chambersburg PA
CBHW030119010526
44116CB00005B/313